When I Die *I'm Going to* HEAVEN
'Cause I've Spent my Time in Hell

When I Die I'm Going to Heaven 'Cause I've Spent my Time in Hell
Copyright © 2013 Barbara Hesselman Kautz, MSN, RN.
2nd edition
All rights reserved.

No part of this book may be used or reproduced in any manner whatsoever without written permission, except in the case of brief quotations embodied in critical articles and reviews. For more information, e-mail all inquiries to info@piscataquapress.com

Published by Piscataqua Press

142 Fleet Street | Portsmouth, New Hampshire 03801 | USA

603.431.2100 | info@piscataquapress.com

Printed in the United States of America
ISBN-13: 978-1-939739-16-2
Library of Congress Control Number: On file with the publisher

Barbara Hesselman Kautz, MSN, RN

When I Die *I'm Going to* HEAVEN *'Cause I've Spent my Time in Hell:*

*A memoir
of my year as
an Army Nurse
in Vietnam*

DEDICATION

To the patients I cared for and the men and women with whom I served in Vietnam, especially my friends Carol Ann Rogers, Carol Konieczny Brown, Susan Lodge Backs, Stephanie Genthon Kilpatrick, and most of all, Joanne Kane Halcomb. Without you I would never have survived that terrible, wonderful, and awful year.

To my family for encouraging me to write this book, and to the people of the University of Southern Maine OLLI Memoir Group for encouraging me to write the hard parts.

And in memory of the late MAJ Theodore Friedhoff, ANC, who taught me how to be a good nurse.

"Better is peace than always war."

The Armed Man

By Karl Jenkins

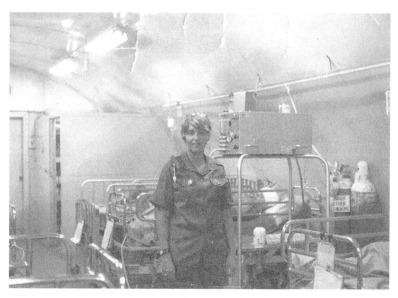

Me & equipment on Ward 5, April 1970

INTRODUCTION

I joined the Army to finance my nursing education shortly after I returned from a year as an American Field Service exchange student, having spent my senior year in high school living with a family in the suburbs of Copenhagen, Denmark. I was eighteen.

The year was 1965, men between the ages of eighteen and thirty-five were eligible for the draft, and President Lyndon Johnson was in the process of sending, what would ultimately be a half-million men to fight communist aggression in Southeast Asia. If asked, most people would not have been able to find Vietnam on a map. They knew the star of the movie "Cat Ballou" as Jane Fonda, Henry's daughter, and not Jane Fonda, war protester.

I spent the first two years of college completing prerequisites to attend the University of Maryland School of Nursing as part of the Army's elite Walter Reed Army Institute of Nursing (WRAIN.) The second two years I spent in clinical internships at Walter Reed Army Hospital in Washington, D.C. Many of the men I cared for as a student were either wounded or sickened in Vietnam. The war became much more than something I saw on the evening news; seeing its effects were an everyday part of my life.

I spent my final semester as a nursing student working on a neurosurgical ward, learning how to manage the care of groups of patients. One of my assignments was to write a description of each patient's day in his medical record. One day my instructor read what I had written about a patient and remarked, "It's so clear you should be a writer." Later, I discovered she meant my handwriting was so clear I should be a writer, but by then I'd had an epiphany: Someday I would become a writer, and if I were to be sent to Vietnam I would write about my experiences there. I even asked my parents to save my letters, which were written journal-style.

Unfortunately, while I was in Vietnam they sold my childhood home, and tossed the letters. Why would their vagabond of a daughter want to keep them?

Over the years, I have asked my friends from Vietnam to share their memories, or help me clarify some of my own. They had better pictures than I, but I quickly discovered that even without my letters I remembered events in far greater detail than they did. Some things, like watching "M*A*S*H" in the Officers' Club were very clear. In others, I remembered only the most basic details. What follows then, is a memoir in the most contemporary definition of the term. The stories are true, even though the details may not be entirely accurate. Most involve, in some way, my closest friends: Joanne, Carol Ann, Stephanie, Carol, and Susan, and a handful of doctors and corpsmen with whom I worked. Whenever possible I have attributed experiences to the correct persons involved. Sometimes, for the ease of story-telling, I have consolidated the actions of several into one person. This is particularly true of the corpsmen with whom I worked. Likewise, I have changed some names, especially of people with whom I no longer have contact. But Joanne, Carol Ann, Susan, Stephanie and Carol are real people whose lives continue to touch mine more than forty years after the events described herein. Any mistakes in the retelling are mine alone.

In 2017, thanks to a perfect storm of problems and errors with the printing of this book, published in 2013, I was given the opportunity to do some revision to the original manuscript. Most were minor, and because I had misplaced some of the pictures, most in this version are either scanned from a copy of the book, or are different than the original. In talking to people about "When I Die…" I have learned that additional descriptions of emotions might improve the overall content. Call this what you want: a revised edition or one with some minor changes. It is still the story of my year as a nurse in Vietnam. Now that fifty years have passed since the worst of the war, it seems fitting, somehow, to revisit the experience.

In Class A uniform shortly before graduation.
May, 1969

Commissioning ceremony. My parents pinning
2LT bars on my epaulets. May, 1969

Chapter 1.
LAMBS TO SLAUGHTER

The Braniff Airlines jet stood on the edge of the tarmac, midway between the Travis Air Force Base terminal and runway. Already on board the big 747 were the pilots and stewardesses, and about twenty non-commissioned and commissioned officers, including five women, all Second Lieutenants in the Army Nurse Corps. We five sat together, three in one row, two in the row behind as if we were pioneer women huddling together inside circling wagons. But there were no wagons, and we weren't settlers; we were nurses on our way to Vietnam.

After twenty minutes, during which we five quietly speculated about the wait, four school buses painted olive drab and stenciled with letters reading *Oakland Army Barracks* pulled up near the plane. One by one, young men uniformly dressed in brand new fatigues, combat boots, and baseball hats stepped off the buses. Commands were given and the men lined up, ready to board the flight.

It was nearing midnight on Tuesday, 17 February 1970 and the tableau unfolding below was made surreal by spotlights used to brighten the area. To a man, those waiting to board the plane looked so young, so inexperienced, and so alike—olive drab lambs being led to slaughter. As I watched them file on board one by one, I wondered how many would get on a plane like this in February 1971 to return home, or, how many would pass through a hospital's doors to eventually be air-evaced out. Or, how many would come home in body bags.

But then I thought my fellow nurses and I were a little like lambs, too. I had no doubt we would still be alive at year's end, but, to a woman, we were all young and inexperienced, out of nursing school less than a year.

And I knew we would see slaughter. A graduate of the Army's elite Walter Reed Army Institute of Nursing, I spent my last two years of college in a series of supervised clinical internships at Walter Reed Army Hospital in Washington, D.C. during the height of the war.

Almost all my patients had been wounded or sickened in Vietnam. I was accustomed to seeing men whose bodies had been shattered in battle or wasted by tropical diseases. I did not know that even big city medical centers like Massachusetts General Hospital rarely had more than a handful of patients recovering from amputated limbs. On average, at Walter Reed, we had more than thirty.

In 1965, when I joined the Army to finance my nursing education, Lyndon Johnson had been the elected president for about nine months, there were about 184,000 men and women stationed in Vietnam, and Jane Fonda was starring in the movie *Cat Ballou*. In 1968—my junior year at Walter Reed—both Robert Kennedy and Martin King were assassinated, and *The War* was becoming increasingly unpopular. Troop levels were at their highest with 536,100 men and women assigned to duty in the war zone.

In Officers' Basic Training in July 1969, I sat in a crowded auditorium filled with new Army nurses, as our instructors completed what might best be described as "a dog and pony show." We viewed recruiting films about nursing in Vietnam, then listened as a career officer and Vietnam veteran described the need for nurses in Vietnam. Her talk was usually followed by a lecture in which another career officer cautioned us against volunteering for duty until we were more experienced. Implicit in their message was the fact that nurses no longer had to volunteer to go to Vietnam. The need had become too great; young women and men routinely received orders for Vietnam without consideration of their experience.

I suspect that, like myself, most of the audience had joined the Army for its generous scholarship programs, without giving much thought to a future that might include combat nursing. Or, as one friend, who had gone to college on a two-year scholarship, put it: "My recruiter lied to me."

When I sat watching my fellow lambs board the plane much had changed from my first encounter with a wounded soldier in the summer of 1967. Richard Nixon was president, troop levels were had been reduced to 475,200, and my fellow country-men were becoming more vocally opposed to our presence in Vietnam.

I was not afraid to go to Vietnam, but simply resigned to the possibility, an attitude I'd developed at Walter Reed. I believed I was better prepared than my companions on that Branff flight because I had already cared for so many wounded men. More importantly, my closest friend from Walter Reed, Joanne Kane, also had orders for Vietnam and would arrive in country about six weeks after me. Wanting to be assigned together we had, on the advice of a friend, taken the daring step of writing to the Chief Nurse of Vietnam explaining our situation, and requesting assignment to the same hospital.

This same friend suggested we ask to be sent to one of the two hospitals at the Army's huge Long Binh Post: the 93rd Evacuation Hospital, a burn center, or the 24th Evac, which specialized in treating men with central nervous system injuries. Both hospitals, each with about 350 beds, could easily absorb two new nurses arriving in country six weeks apart.

Now a twenty-four-hour flight across the Pacific awaited us. We would stop in Honolulu for fuel and then again in Manila, where we would change planes. Our destination was Bien Hoa Air Force Base, about 30 miles north east of Saigon and six miles north of Long Binh Post, also home to the Headquarters for all the Army's medically related corps. It was here, in the office of the Chief Nurse of Vietnam that the following twelve months would be laid before us.

When the plane finally entered Vietnamese airspace everyone leaned toward the nearest window, anxious for our first sight of Vietnam. We could see green below: lush, deep green peppered with enormous brick red craters created by bombs dropped from B-52s.

After a few moments I got up to use the bathroom. A startled stewardess pushed me back into my seat.

"But I have to go to the bathroom."

When I Die I'm Going to HEAVEN

The Hospital from the air

"Not until we're on the ground." She locked the seatbelt firmly around my middle as the pitch of the plane's engines changed and we dove toward the airbase below.

As soon as we landed school buses careened toward the plane, abruptly stopping just below the gangways. These buses were painted Air Force Blue and had steel mesh on the inside of every window. Young men in jungle fatigues and Air Force insignia, armed with pistols and machine guns boarded the plane and began barking out orders.

We were to exit the plane as quickly and orderly as possible. We were not to touch the windows in the bus. We were not to worry about our belongings. They would be delivered to us at our destination: the 90th Replacement Company, just outside the gates of Long Binh Post.

"But I have to use the toilet," I protested.

"It's too dangerous here. You'll have to wait."

Like the rest of the flight's lambs I hurried off the plane and raced for the bus. As I stepped onto the tarmac I immediately noticed several things. When I left Pennsylvania it was snowing. In San Francisco the weather had been in the low 50°s. But as I dashed to the bus I couldn't help but notice the heat and humidity. It was overpowering. Like suddenly being dropped into a huge sauna with no exit. The other thing I noticed was the smell. It was sour yet oddly exotic, a mix of burning waste products and Vietnamese cooking. It seemed to settle in my nose where it would continue to capture my olfactory nerves for the ensuing 365 days.

As soon as we arrived at the 90th Replacement Company we were hustled into a large theater to see a movie about turning our greenbacks over to military authorities in favor of the legal tender for the U.S. Military in Vietnam: MPCs, or Military Pay Currency. Paying with US dollars would further weaken an already damaged Vietnamese economy, we were told. Better to use the MPC.

Then we five nurses were pulled aside and taken to get the fatigues, "boonie hats", and jungle specific combat boot we were to wear for the next year.

During this time I asked twice about using the latrine. But there was only one bathroom on all the 90th Replacement Company specifically designated for use by servicewomen and it was on the opposite side of post, next to the temporary quarters for female officers.

"You'll have to wait Lieutenant. If we hurry we can get you over to the Chief Nurse's Office today. That'll shorten your time here."

I didn't have the nerve to pull rank. Instead, I piled into a jeep with my fellow nurses and was whisked across the space separating the 90th Replacement Company from Long Binh Post.

We kept up this breakneck pace, bouncing along pockmarked roads until we reached Headquarters. In my mind's eye I could see the headlines in the Greensburg (PA) Tribune Review: *Local Nurse Dies of Ruptured Bladder Upon Arrival in Vietnam.*

Our destination was a long, two storied concrete block affair. Its insides were painted a drag green, the floors covered in brown linoleum so that it resembled any other military office building on any other Army post across the world. The driver led us upstairs and into the office of COL Patricia Murphy, the Chief Nurse for all Army nurses in Vietnam.

Her office was much like any other office for a senior officer on any other Army post. As we entered the room COL Murphy looked up from her large desk, piled high with papers. With short cut dark hair streaked with a few strands of gray, and dressed in fatigues and combat boots she looked a lot like other Colonels I had met before. Except she seemed to ignore the Army's interdiction against long fingernails, for she had them and they were painted a bright red. To her left was a small sitting area furnished with several chairs arranged in a semi-circle. On the wall hung a large map of Vietnam.

After appropriate greetings, COL Murphy began to launch into what I am sure was a familiar speech, welcoming us to Vietnam, citing how important our service would be. After a sentence or two I timidly raised my hand.

"What is it Lieutenant?" COL Murphy snapped, unused to interruptions by very junior officers.

"I have needed to use the bathroom since we entered Vietnamese airspace and no one will let me go. May I please have permission to use the toilet?" My bladder hurt so much from the ride from the 90th Replacement I thought I might cry and if I did my tears would surely contain uric acid.

COL Murphy roared with laughter. "It's the fourth door to the right down the hall."

Relieved of my liquid burden, I returned to the Chief Nurse's air-conditioned office and slid into my chair. As I did, COL Murphy ran through a list of things we five should be mindful of during our time in country:

1. Stay on post.
2. Don't take any unauthorized rides in jeeps or helicopters.
3. Don't fraternize with the enlisted men.
4. Don't fraternize with the married men.
5. Make the best of the year to come.

Each of us had conversed with predecessors from our former duty assignments. We knew these cautions were coming and accepted them as reasonable advice. We also knew we would probably break some of the rules, especially those about staying on post and taking unauthorized rides in jeeps or helicopters. Everyone hitch-hiked on large posts like Long Binh. Unless you had a driver's license and access to the motor pool it was key to getting around.

It was impossible not to become friends with helicopter pilots, and by extension, stay out of the air. As a group, helicopter pilots were key to our existence. They brought us wounded, staying at the hospital for a hot meal or long enough to find out how an evacuee was doing. Socially, they were our equals, for like us, they were mostly college educated, junior officers, and single.

Nevertheless, COL Murphy's advice was wise advice. Fraternizing with an enlisted man, no matter his status in civilian life, was grounds for official censure. Fraternizing with a married man, and thus most of the doctors, could only bring heartache. And flying in helicopters carried with it a certain degree of danger. Of the seven women soldiers to die in Vietnam only one was killed in the line of duty. One nurse probably committed suicide, another died of a Fever of Unknown Origin (FUO.) One nurse had been killed in a plane crash; the other three had been joyriding in helicopters.

Her lecture complete, COL Murphy drew our attention to the large wall map behind her.

On it were stick pins indicating the locations of all the medical units in Vietnam where Army nurses could be assigned. Next to each pin was the name of the hospital printed in large black letters; beneath it were three sets of numbers: nurses presently on duty, current vacancies, and the number of nurses set to DEROS (Date of Estimated Rotation Overseas—the day we would return home) within the next month. The map showed vacancies just about everywhere but particularly at the 3rd Field Hospital in Saigon. Some of the more desirable hospitals like the one near the beaches of Vung Tau on the South China Sea, had been closed as the Army slowly handed military control over to the South Vietnamese.

If Joanne weren't joining me I might have asked to go to the 18th Surgical Hospital, the closest hospital to the DMZ (Demilitarized Zone between North and South Vietnam) even though it was also the hospital most in harm's way. But the 18th Surg was small, too small to guarantee we could be together.

The one place I knew I did not want to go was the 3rd Field. It might have been in Saigon, and thus offer an opportunity to learn about South Vietnam's exotic capitol, but the 3rd Field was the Army's showcase hospital in Vietnam. The nurses there wore starched white uniforms, white shoes and stockings, and nurses' caps. In tropically humid Vietnam, with the mud and mess of an accompanying rainy season, this made no sense to me. I would rather go somewhere nurses wore jungle fatigues.

COL Murphy looked us over. She could have gone down the line and assigned each of us to a hospital most in need of nurses. But she did not. She let the numbers sink in for a few moments, then said, "I would like to see two or three of you go to the 3rd Field. As you can see they have several nurses going home in the next few weeks. It has a lot to offer. Nice nurses' quarters and the opportunity to see Saigon. I'll give you a moment to think about it."

I tentatively raised my hand.

"What is it now, Lieutenant?" COL Murphy asked.

"I am the nurse who wrote you about being stationed with my friend Joanne Kane."

"Oh yes, I remember who you are now."

"I was assured you wouldn't mind."

I thought quickly, knowing I had to seize the moment. Another friend was already at the 93rd Evac, a burn unit. I knew nothing about caring for burn patients. I did know something about caring for men with neurological injuries. No matter where she went Joanne would be in the ICU.

"The 24th Evac."

With these three words I set in motion a number of events that would forever alter our lives.

The Hospital sign

Chapter 2.
WELCOME TO THE 24ᵀᴴ EVAC

As soon as our driver returned us to the 90th Replacement Company, he grabbed my belongings and hurried me back to the jeep.

"What's the rush?" I asked, content with the thought of spending a night in the female officers' quarters, a large open room with screens instead of windows, and cots enveloped in mosquito netting. I would have liked an evening with my fellow newbies (Vietnam speak for someone who had been in Vietnam less than a couple of months) before getting to the serious part of my stay.

"It's almost 1600 (4 PM)," he replied. "Your friend going up north will have to wait until we can get her on a flight up there, and it's too late to drive to and from Saigon before dark. But the 24th Evac is just down the road."

And so another jeep ride, albeit a short one. The driver pulled up to a large sign bearing the name and insignia of the 24th Evac: a red cross surrounded by a "ŏ", meant to symbolize a helicopter's rotors.

Next to it was yet another headquarters, this one a medium sized wooden building with offices for the Commanding Officer, LTC Leo LeBlanc, MD and another for his wife Lillian, who was Chief Nurse.

LTC Lillian LeBlanc sat at her desk, which was a little smaller but just as cluttered as COL Murphy's had been. Tall and slender with serious eyes and graying blonde hair, LTC LeBlanc looked tired and worn. She and I went through a welcoming and lecture similar to the one I had heard at headquarters. Then LTC LeBlanc looked at *her* chart, which was not of Vietnam but of the 13 wards and Emergency Room that made up the 24th Evac. Similar sets of numbers were listed below the name of each ward.

"Do you have a preference where you would like to work?"

"One of the surgical wards, or the Recovery Room. I was in the Recovery Room at Letterman." But the numbers on the board were not in my favor.

"I don't need anyone in the RR at the moment. I have two nurses from the medical units DEROSing in the next two weeks. And I always need people on Ward 5, the neurosurgical unit."

I had already been warned not to volunteer for Ward 5, which was considered the worst place in the hospital in which to work. Its death rate was higher than that of the ER and ORs combined. But I hadn't come all this way to take care of guys with malaria and hepatitis.

"Well," I gulped, "I did my senior rotation at Walter Reed on the neuro unit. You may as well assign me to Ward 5."

She smiled, pleased.

The 24th Evac was laid out in the shape of a giant squared U with its little tail off to the right. At the base of the U were the chapel, pharmacy, and Red Cross office. Admitting, the ER, lab, and X-ray made up the little tail. Ward 1, which was both a pre-op stabilization area and the recovery room, and six operating rooms—two per hut, occupied a total of four Quonsets next to the ER. Ward 2 on the far side of the operating rooms was the surgical intensive care unit, next to it were Wards 3, and 4, both general surgical units for men whose condition did not warrant the constant vigilance of intensive care.

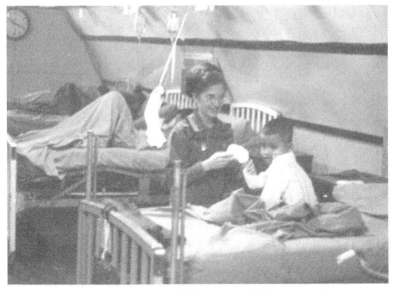

Susan with Vietnamese child

The Quonset huts on the left side of the hospital comprised one ward after another: 5 and 6 for neurosurgery, 7 and 8 for medical patients, 9 and 10 for orthopedics, 13 and 14 for convalescing patients, and 15 for patients, many of whom were Vietnamese children, with maxillofacial injuries or congenital malformations caused by the prolific use of the defoliant Dioxin (Agent Orange). Wards 11 and 12 had been taken over by physical therapy.

Beyond Ward 15 stood five one story wooden buildings with real windows. Four of these were quarters for the junior-most single female nurses and Red Cross volunteers, and one, curiously set between Hooches 2 and 3, was the Officer's Club.

While each ward on both sides of the hospital was contained within its own Quonset, the entire length of the left side of the hospital was connected, to those on each side by a short passageway that held the nurses' station, reference books, cubby holes for our mail, and real bathrooms with sinks, showers, and flush toilets. I could stand at the nurses' station in the middle of Ward 5 and see nurses sitting at their desks down the entire length of that side of the hospital. At night the wards would be dark except for lights at each ward's nurses' station, and Ward 5, where we never turned off the lights.

Covered walkways ran the length of both sides of the hospital just in front of the mess hall a second walkway bisected the open area between the two flanks of the hospital, another convenience during rainy season. None of the Quonsets had windows; instead each window space held an air conditioning unit. This would turn out to be one of the best things about the 24th Evac.

My duffel bag, suitcase, and newly issued jungle fatigues lay in a neat pile on the floor of my new room in Hooch 3. It was about 10'x10' with a single metal dresser and wardrobe, both painted an indeterminate drab color, not quite green, not quite tan. A metal cot held a real mattress, and above it was a window, nailed shut. Yet, much to my amazement, the room was cold, air-conditioned by a large cooling duct cut into the wall above my bed.

I would learn later that some genius—and I mean that sincerely—had decided to extend air-conditioning to the nurses' quarters when they were installing central air in the operating rooms years earlier. I would come to bless that person many times during the year, especially on blazingly hot days when I needed to sleep between twelve-hour night shifts. But on that first night I could not sleep. Even with my quilt, a wool blanket, and my rain coat covering me I was freezing.

After surveying the room, I contemplated my pile of belongings then looked at my watch. Dinner time, and I was hungry. Had they fed us lunch on the flight from Manila? It had been so long, the changes in time zones so confusing, I couldn't remember.

The mess hall was a large wooden structure divided in two: one side for the enlisted men, another for the officers. I quickly learned the Mess Hall at the 24th Evac prepared reasonably good food. Nothing extravagant, but rather a steady supply of basics like roast beef, pork chops, mashed potatoes, frozen vegetables, and spaghetti. For dinner there were always two menu choices, and plenty of milk. It came in regular waxed eight-ounce containers but did not taste like it had just come from an American milk processing plant. Perhaps it was boiled or even irradiated because it had an odd taste to it; still, I found it more palatable than powdered milk.

There was always homemade bread, coffee, and an enormous tub of peanut butter placed on a small table between the two rooms, always available in case anyone got hungry between meals. And, oh yes, midnight breakfast served to the night shift between 2300 and 0100 hrs.

At that first dinner, sitting alone in the Officers' Mess, I noticed a familiar face. No, it was not someone from my nursing class at Walter Reed but rather Nora Hoffman, a young woman from my home town. Her sister and I had often sat together on the long bus ride home from junior high. Back then she'd been in senior high, and thus on a different schedule than her sister and me, but Nora sometimes rode the bus home with us. I knew she had been accepted into nursing school, and during those rides I had quizzed her about her plans. I admired her and was a bit surprised my mother, who worked in the local post office, hadn't told me Nora was in Vietnam.

Excitedly, I said hello. Nora, who worked as an operating room nurse, did not remember me, nor did she seem interested in getting to know me. A short-timer (Vietnam speak for someone nearing the end of her yearlong tour of duty,) she was burnt out and more than ready to go home. Becoming reacquainted with a junior-high friend of her kid sister, especially one newly arrived from the world (more Vietnam speak for anywhere other than Vietnam), held no appeal. I ate my dinner alone. A few nurses eyed me curiously, a few more said "hello," but it was nearing shift change and their focus was not on the newbie with the short blonde hair, who rumor had it, had actually volunteered for Ward 5.

Shift change occurred while I was trying to unpack. Two of my neighbors, Sandy and Doreen introduced themselves, welcoming me to the 24th Evac, but they did not linger. Each had plans for the evening. Change of shift report began at 1845 and took a good half hour. The entire post lived under a curfew beginning at 2200 hrs. Little time in which to legally conduct a social life.

And there was a social life at both the 24th Evac and Long Binh Post. Since it was a huge post there were many Officers' Clubs scattered about Long Binh. Some held excellent reputations for serving good steaks and stiff drinks. And then there was "Loon Foon's," a Chinese restaurant no more than a quarter mile walk from the hospital. Off duty, we were not required to be in uniform, and I would soon learn how much a commodity we American women were. Having a round eyed (non-Oriental) date in civilian clothes accompany him to an O club was, for many an officer, an enviable triumph.

As I unpacked my belongings I made plans for the next day. In the morning I would get a second, more thorough tour of the hospital, discovering the locations of the helicopter pad, the Agent Orange dump, the morgue, the bunkers, the men's quarters, and a small hospital for prisoners of war staffed by people assigned to the 24th Evac. I would learn that I was expected to employ a Vietnamese civilian, a mammasan, who, for about $7 in MPCs a week, would make my bed, clean my room, polish my boots, and wash and iron my uniforms.

I would be given a tour of the surrounding area, including nearby post exchanges and the swimming pool across the street, behind the Agent Orange dump, and finally, I would be given the opportunity to take my fatigues to a civilian tailor who would hem and iron them, and sew onto the blouse the appropriate patches indicating that I, Barbara Hesselman, was a Second Lieutenant (2LT) in the Army Nurse Corp stationed at the 24th Evacuation Hospital in the Republic of South Vietnam.

As the week progressed I would learn that we worked twelve hour shifts 7-7, six days—or nights—a week, and longer if dictated by the census. I would learn that Ward 5's reputation was indeed accurate, for Ward 5 was thought to be such a terrible place to work its nurses were given the opportunity to transfer to another ward after six months. I would learn that while most of the patients on Ward 6 were confused and ambulatory, and generally pleasant to care for, most of the staff preferred taking care of the GORKED (for God Only Really Knows the extent of brain damage) patients who were so seriously wounded they needed constant care if they were to have a chance for what would certainly be a "new normal" life.

And, I would learn that, depending on one's willingness to go along with the absurd, a lot of the Ward 5 staff believed it was possessed by a sprite named Mighty Ralph Gooyami, whose capricious pulling of the unseen strings of fate could make a patient take a turn for the better or transform a normal night shift into hell. And I would learn the corpsmen spent an inordinate amount of time scrubbing the floor with water laced with oil of wintergreen to cover the ward's omnipresent odor, which I eventually figured out was the smell of decaying flesh.

This view of the hospital from the air was taken from the opposite end of the hospital than the diagram.

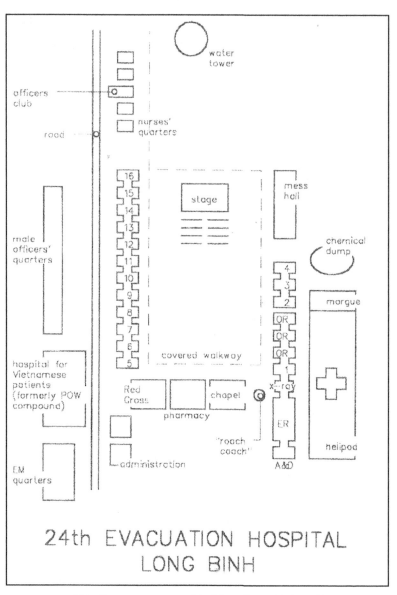

This diagram was created by Mary Reynolds Powell, with my help, for her excellent book, "A World of Hurt."

Chapter 3.
STANDING ON THE BRINK

The nurses *really* in charge of the 24th Evac were LTC LeBlanc's two assistants: MAJ Margaret Kelly and MAJ Margaret Lewis, "The Two Pegs." They were nothing alike, even if they shared the same first name. MAJ Margaret Kelly was tall and thin, with wispy blonde hair. I have never been able to estimate a person's age by her facial features alone. MAJ Kelly could easily have been 30 or 40, but she seemed older, more settled than her counterpart. This was her second year-long tour in Vietnam. We all knew "lifers" who volunteered for more than one year in the war zone, and most of the junior nurses thought they were crazy. However, in MAJ Kelly's case it was easily explainable: her husband, a senior non-commissioned officer (NCO) was assigned elsewhere on Long Binh Post. She had chosen to stay with her man, even if meant another year in Vietnam, and for this I admired her. How she managed to break the Army's rules about fraternizing with enlisted men, even senior NCOs, was a mystery. In an emergency she was calm and quiet, given to offering serious advice.

MAJ Peg Lewis was her polar opposite. Of medium height and build, with thick, dark hair that curled just above her collar, Peg Lewis was a go-getter, a problem-solver. I sensed this about her that first morning when she found me sitting in the mess hall, waiting to begin my year in Vietnam. And she would prove it time and again in the way she took charge either when things did not go the way we expected or whenever quick action was needed.

On that first morning Peg Lewis took me to the appropriate office where I handed over my personnel file, the official record of my time in the Army I had carried with me from San Francisco. We then visited the Vietnamese tailor, who helped me choose the appropriate insignia for my uniform and suggested the appropriate length for my fatigue pants. Then she showed me the hospital's tiny Post Exchange, where I bought cigarettes. Finally, she took me on a second, more detailed tour of the hospital, even giving me a peek into the interior of one of the operating rooms.

As we walked through the hospital she filled in details about life at the 24th Evac that had nothing to do with being a nurse: how to send a letter home, the time mail was delivered, the location on the FM dial for Armed Forces Vietnam Radio, when malaria pills were handed out, how to set up a bank account on post, and how much money in MPCs I would need during a typical month.

MAJ Lewis was pleasant and friendly, but I was a bit wary of her. In all probability she, too, was a "lifer"—someone who intended to make being an Army nurse her profession, and that alone made me suspicious. My nursing instructors at Walter Reed were career Army nurses: all excellent nurses with advanced practice degrees. Most had also kind and friendly. But at that moment, anxious just to get through the year, I couldn't understand the motivation of someone who chose to be a nurse in the Army for her entire career.

After lunch we returned to the Vietnamese tailor who handed me my uniform blouses with the Nurse Corps insignia, the black and gold embroidered Second Lieutenant bars, and my properly spelled surname in all the right places. Thus, finished with "in-processing" I thought I might be given the rest of the day to unpack and unwind. But that was not the case. Instead, MAJ Lewis took me to Ward 5 where I was to meet my fellow nurses and corpsmen, and my new head nurse, CPT Theodore, "Ted," Friedhoff.

Introductions complete, Ted sat me down and began describing in detail what I should expect on Wards 5 and 6, generally referred to simply as Ward 5. After completing orientation, I would be scheduled for six 12-hour day shifts a week, then be given a day off before rotating to nights. When I completed the sixth night, I would be given a "sleep day," followed by a day off before rotating back to days in a repeating cycle that would occasionally give me part of a weekend off. Not that it mattered. In war, one day is much like another—including weekends, nights, and holidays.

We followed a concept of providing care called "Team Nursing," which meant nurses would be expected to care for all patients on the ward, but would have different roles, such as medication or dressing nurse. As he talked, Ted stressed the importance of being part of the team if we were to do our very best for the men in our care.

The evening before—my first night in Vietnam—one of the other nurses in my hooch warned me about CPT Friedhoff. "You know," she said, scowling, "he's pretty new to Ward 5. I hear they brought him in because his predecessor couldn't control the corpsmen. He's a hard core hard ass."

I quickly learned nothing could be further from the truth. To be sure CPT Friedhoff, known to the nurses as Ted, valued discipline, but he valued teamwork more. Placed in charge of a group of young adults still on the brink of developing their own ideas about professional behavior, he led by example. His kindness and insight into others' problems and how they affected our ability to do our work—not to mention our morale—made him one of the best head nurses with whom I have ever worked.

Although he was quiet, Ted had a good sense of humor and did not run nearly as tight a ship as my hooch mate had indicated. More importantly, he was a good listener, who more than once steered his younger nurses onto a path that both professional and ethical. Ted was willing to share his thoughts on the Army, on nursing, and on leadership with the junior officers in his charge.

I once asked Ted how old he was, and he prevaricated. His curly brown hair was streaked with gray, and so I guessed he was closer to 40 than 30. He had not gone to nursing school straight out of high school and he had spent some time—I never knew how much—as a civilian nurse. When we met he'd been in the Army for about seven years, and, given the tempo of the times, he should have been a Major.

Climbing the "Rank Ladder" is of extreme importance to career military men and women, whether officers or enlisted. Given that Ted had been in the Army long enough to be a Major, I got the impression that he had made his share of mistakes early in his career and had lost opportunities for promotion as a result.

He never elaborated and rarely talked about his personal life, although I did learn he was a fellow Pennsylvanian and was divorced. It didn't seem to matter to him whether he got out of the Army as a Major or a Lieutenant Colonel. What mattered was Ward 5. He seemed damn sure *his* nurses would learn to become effective leaders.

At my first duty assignment, Letterman Army Hospital in San Francisco, I had pushed to be assigned to the Recovery Room, even though the head nurse was a bone-crushing bitch who thoroughly disliked new graduates, especially those from WRAIN. Both my chief nurse and supervisor had advised against going to the Recovery Room, and instead offered me a slot in the newborn nursery. Knowing that Letterman was a prized posting for Vietnam returnees I thought my chances of going to Vietnam were better than someone assigned to a less prestigious facility.

My superiors were right to try to protect me from her nastiness. But I wanted to learn surgical nursing, and had opted for the R.R. and its head nurse, who, indeed, was a bone-crushing bitch. Her treatment of me was so bad I was content to get orders to go to Vietnam.

[When she arrived in Vietnam midway through my year I threatened to ask for a transfer to another hospital if she wound up at the 24th Evac. Luckily—for me—she did not.]

Ted could not have been more different than "The Bitch," and for this I was grateful.

Ward 5's corpsmen were led by the "Ward Sergeant," or "Ward Master," Sergeant Major William Reynolds. A tall, solidly built African American, SGM Reynolds looked like he belonged on a football field, not in an Army Hospital riding roughshod over a bunch of young corpsmen with no interest whatsoever in making the Army their career. He was more a disciplinarian than Ted, probably because he had to be.

More than anyone on Ward 5 SGM Reynolds seemed most

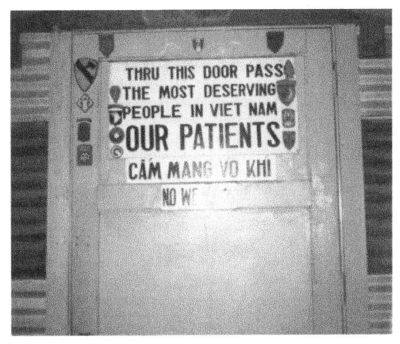

acutely aware of the differences in rank, particularly between the nurses and corpsmen. Perhaps it had something to do with being one of the few black men at the 24th Evac; more likely it had to do with the fact that SGM Reynolds had risen through the enlisted ranks, earning his leadership role the hard way. No one called him by his first name. Not even Ted.

Technically, his Military Occupation Specialty (MOS) was "91C"—that of a Licensed Practical Nurse back in the world. But SGM Reynolds spent no time caring for patients. Rather, he saw to it that we had sufficient supplies for our patient load, helped arrange transport whenever the wounded were ready to go home, scheduled the duty roster for the corpsmen, and made sure the place was clean. The afternoon before, when I first set eyes on Ward 5, SGM Reynolds was one of the men scrubbing the floor.

Years after I left Vietnam I heard a joke about a doctor who died and went to Hell. There he was given a choice between working in a never ending Intensive Care Unit in which bells and alarms went off constantly, or sitting in an ever-lasting medical records room signing orders and completing progress notes. I loved this joke because on Ward 5 I had already lived it.

My Hell was an endlessly repeating world of hanging IVs, flashing bright lights into young men's eyes, changing dressings, suctioning tracheotomies, checking on ventilator function, and changing the position of spinal cord patients every two hours.

Dressing changes were long and painful and had to be repeated two or three times a day. IVs had to run on time, pupils needed to be checked often to see if there were changes in the way they reacted to light—an early indicator of worsening brain damage. There was also pain to be inflicted by performing a kind of pinching motion on various parts of the bodies, an indicator of what part of the brain was most damaged.

We placed men with spinal cord injuries on a special bed called a Stryker Frame. This was a narrow stretcher-like contraption with a top and bottom. Because a patient with spinal cord injuries could not move, the Stryker frame allowed us to change his position by sandwiching a man between a top and bottom frame, flipping him from back to belly then to back again every two hours to keep him from developing bedsores. This was the most important thing we could do for a man unable to move—or feel—below the damage to the spinal cord.

To get a sense of what it felt like to be repositioned on a Stryker frame, staff members were encouraged to be flipped at least once, so we could better understand what our spinal cord patients had to endure. When it was my turn I discovered it was dizzying and uncomfortable, an experience I was happy never to have to repeat.

Our days then were governed by a certain rhythm and routine. Although many of our tasks were repetitive, we could never let down our guard. After injury, all soft tissue, regardless of location, swells as part of the body's normal response to being damaged. In most parts of the body this type of inflammation holds no serious, long term consequence. But for brain and spinal cord patients, tissue swelling can cause more damage as the brain bumps into the skull, or the spinal cord into the spinal column. The result: even more destruction. Failing to identify changes in brain function spelled doom for patients who might otherwise recover to lead normal lives. I always tried to keep this thought in mind, never allowing myself to become complacent.

The Quonset hut housing Ward 5 was a large open area with only three small enclosed spaces: two storage areas in the front of the hut, and the medication room near the back door. Standing at the entrance to the medication room I could look down the length of the ward at a lane created in the space between two rows of beds facing each other. In all there were about 20 beds with room for four to six Stryker frames. Running along both sides of the hut were pieces of metal tubing painted the same dull shade as the walls. These were for hanging IV bottles— much easier than each bed having its own IV pole.

Ventilators, equipment for cooling blankets, and other paraphernalia occupied spaces around some of the beds. I have a few black and white pictures of Ward 5 taken early during my year in Vietnam. In it I am a tall, slender, attractive young woman standing in front of this astonishing compilation of equipment. That the photograph should be in black and white seems somehow more appropriate than if it were in color, for my memories of the Ward itself, despite the endless pain and suffering inflicted there are flat, drab, and gray, as though I have purposely washed away the color of blood, shit, and urine, pain, frustration, and ceil blue hospital sheets from my memory.

Because Ward 5 was a de facto intensive care unit most of our patients had multiple injuries with fractured limbs, open facial, neck, and abdominal wounds, and could easily have qualified as patients on any other surgical unit in the hospital—if it hadn't been for their head injuries.

On most days Ward 5 was staffed by two or three nurses, Ward 6 with another nurse or two. Although he had administrative duties, Ted also helped out as needed. The corpsmen were responsible for taking routine vital signs, usually every hour; one nurse was responsible for mixing and hanging the intravenous fluid that ran through every patient's veins, and another nurse, sometimes two took on the responsibility of changing patients' dressings. Like a conductor, yet another nurse—Ted often filled this role—made sure things ran smoothly, observations were charted, and changes in patients' status reported.

For the nurses there was little difference between the day and night shift routines. Although we dimmed the lights on Ward 6, whose patients were mostly concussion victims, we kept the overhead lights blazing on Ward 5 day and night because we needed the light to carefully observe men, and sometimes women and children, for changes in brain function. It must have been disconcerting for the few men in our care whose normal circadian rhythms had not been disrupted by their injuries.

For the corpsmen, night shifts were busy, for this was when they replaced dirty sheets with clean, bathed patients, cleansed or changed the catheters used to drain urine from bladders and empty catheter bags.

On Ward 5 our patients lay naked on their beds, covered only by a sheet. We didn't clothe the men because most of them were unable to assist us with this most basic of human actions; and we didn't feed patients because they were too sick. After a few days on Ward 5 few men vomited or were incontinent of feces. They had nothing left in their intestinal tracts to digest.

Although I was a Walter Reed graduate I had no preconceived notions about what the coming year would bring. I was still too young, too green, and too in awe that I, an arm chair World War II history buff, had somehow landed in the middle of a war of my own. Thanks to Walter Reed I knew there would be no glamour, as portrayed in one of my favorite movies, *So Proudly We Hail,* starring Claudette Colbert as an Army Nurse in the Philippines.

I hoped the people I was meeting would be easy to work with. I hoped I would be able to pull my weight and earn my coworkers respect. I hoped I would not despair too deeply over the hours I would spend with the brain injured. I thought I had no illusions; I had seen enough brain damage, spoken to enough nurse Vietnam veterans to know I was indeed facing a year of hell.

One of the things Ted had handed me during that first meeting was a DEROS (Date of Estimated Rotation Overseas) Calendar: a picture of Snoopy as the Red Barron, his body, dog house, and scarf parceled into 365 rectangles: one for each day I would spend in Vietnam. As I tacked my calendar onto an empty piece of wall, next to everyone else's, I prayed the coming year would be tolerable. My mood was more of resignation than of despair. I still didn't know enough of what being at the 24th Evac would be like to fashion an opinion on *how* I should feel. I sensed that what I would most need to learn was how to endure.

But in those early days on Ward 5, my focus, of necessity, was of learning what I would need to know to become a good neuro-nurse. Eventually I would be able to recognize subtle changes in patients' conditions and learn to act on them with speed and confidence. But in the beginning, and in spite of my time on a neurosurgical unit at Walter Reed, I was as green, and quite possibly as dangerous, as a private on his first day on patrol gingerly holding onto his loaded rifle.

Chapter 4.
ACTS OF TORTURE

On my third day in country I began the process of learning more of Ward 5's routines by shadowing Lindy, the nurse assigned to administer medications and hang IVs that day.

The medication room, at the back of the Ward, was little more than a crude plywood enclosure. Bottles of IV fluid, boxes of dried penicillin awaiting reconstitution, and an enormous jar of cotton balls soaking in rubbing alcohol lined the room's make-shift shelves. A full-sized refrigerator filled with pre-mixed bottles of antibiotic laced IV fluid stood against one wall. A long plywood counter with two kitchen cabinets hanging above it stood on the wall next to the door. One cabinet could be locked. It held narcotics like Demerol and morphine and the anti-seizure drug Phenobarbital. But unless a patient was seizing we rarely used the medications in this cabinet. In 1970, medical standards for providing treatment to brain damaged patients strongly discouraged the use of central nervous system depressants, including narcotics.

Today, neurologically injured patients are often placed on a ventilator and given drugs to induce coma, with the belief that this treatment aids in the recovery of damaged tissue, putting the brain to rest so it could heal. But in 1970, coma was to be feared. Comatose patients had more brain damage than those without. And so, we worked to reverse coma as quickly as possible. And our patients suffered. Even if they were somewhat awake they received no pain medication for dressing changes. No morphine to ease respiratory distress. No valium to hold off seizures or relax muscle spasms.

Perhaps most of our patients never knew there were medications available to ease their agony; many *were* comatose. But for those who knew we were consciously inflicting pain we must have seemed like evil ogres, not angels of mercy.

The second cabinet held a variety of medications we used periodically. The most frequently employed medication was mannitol, a powerful sugar based diuretic that could remove excess water from cerebrospinal fluid. There were also large stock bottled of pills like Ampicillin and Ritalin, which, in 1970 was not a controlled substance.

After showing me where medications were stored, Lindy began explaining the system for mixing and hanging alternating bottles of fluid containing a witch's brew of either 5% dextrose in water (D5W) mixed with 20,000,000 units of penicillin or 5% dextrose in Lactated Ringers (D5LR—an IV fluid containing necessary electrolytes) mixed with 2 grams of the antibiotic Chloromycetin. When I tell people today what we used for antibiotics in Vietnam they are dumbfounded by the doses and the drugs of choice. Both antibiotic doses were enormous; Chloromycetin had such terrible side effects its use in the US was limited. But in Vietnam we needed to use every possible tool at our disposal. The rich soil of a Vietnamese rice paddy, fertilized by human waste, created a truly frightening bacterial soup in which men on patrol routinely stepped.

The day medication nurse was responsible for adding the required antibiotic to enough bottles of intravenous fluid to last until the following morning. So, Lindy showed me how to pre-mix and store the bottles, and how to fashion a crude timing tape, using ½ inch wide adhesive tape, marking them in 100 cc/hour intervals, which in turn would enable me to more easily see if an IV was running at the correct rate. This, too, was an important part of my job. Let an IV run too slowly and the patient might suffer from the side effects of dehydration, too fast and his brain tissue might swell even more.

As Lindy continued her explanation I was having trouble following her, for directly across from the medication room lay one of the loudest patients I had ever heard.

"Oh, God, oh God, you're hurting me," the young man screamed, his voice reverberating off the metal walls of the Quonset hut.

"Shut up soldier, and lie still," an unknown voice commanded.

"Oh shit, that hurt. What the fuck are you doing to me?"

Realizing that she was no match for the screaming patient, Lindy dragged me out into the middle of the ward.

"Let's check the IVs," she said. Instead, we stood, transfixed, watching a battle among the dressing nurse, her assistant—a medical corpsman—and our loud patient over his dressing change. The nurse and corpsman were winning, but only because they outnumbered the patient.

His name was Jimmy Ray, a 19-year-old, freckle-faced kid, from a small town in Tennessee. A week earlier he'd been on patrol when his platoon was ambushed, killing several of his comrades.

The radio operator, carrying more than 60 pounds of equipment and supplies, Jimmy Ray had been bringing up the rear. He'd had just enough time to un-sling the radio from his back and call for help before he was hit.

Jimmy Ray belonged in a bed in the middle of the Quonset hut, where he could more easily be observed for changes in his condition. But Jimmy Ray was in the back because no one had expected him to live. Placing him out of view had been standard procedure: the staff's role was to provide basic care until the young man from Tennessee died.

Only Jimmy Ray did not die.

He still lay in the same bed at the back of the ward, directly across from the medication room. His good arm was tied down so he could not pick at his dressings, his fractured extremities encased in half casts covered in gauze. For the first week after he was wounded Jimmy Ray had been in a deep coma, unresponsive to our routine poking and prodding. But now he was beginning to wake up. His mental status fluctuated without reason between semi-comatose to conscious-but-confused. On this particular morning, Jimmy Ray, whose long, muscular body filled the entire bed, bucked on the bed, fighting his tormentors.

The unknown voice I had heard chastising Jimmy Ray belonged to one of our most capable and intense corpsmen, PFC Adam P.

Zakowski, who everyone called Zak. Later Zak would claim that Mighty Ralph had saved Jimmy Ray. But, on this February morning I had yet to be introduced to Zak or Jimmy Ray, or to Mighty Ralph.

Like Jimmy Ray, Zak was 19. And, like Jimmy Ray he was tall and muscular. Zak sported a bushy blonde mustache that gave him a certain air of authority. In many ways, he was the ring leader of the corpsmen. Not all the enlisted men responded to SGM Reynolds's leadership, but everyone—even most of the nurses—looked up to Zak.

From the south side of Chicago, Adam Zakowski was smart, insightful, and sarcastic.

Battle hardened by four months in the field and another three on Ward 5, he did not suffer fools. Period. He could spot a patient's change in condition as fast as any nurse, and he was not shy about giving his opinion on everything from the running of Ward 5 to the height of the learning curve each new nurse brought with her to the 24th Evac. In short, Adam Zakowski had done it all and seen it all. To get along well with Zak you had to earn his respect.

"Oh God, oh God, you're hurting me!" Jimmy Ray screamed again while Zak held Jimmy Ray's arm for the nurse as she unwound the rolls of saturated bandage covering Jimmy Ray's arm. Then she ripped dried gauze from the opened frag wounds, pulling away decaying tissue from the open sore in a process we called *debriding the wound*.

"Shut up, and let's get this over with," Zak instructed Jimmy Ray.

"Please, please, please, you're hurting me!" Jimmy Ray cried again as the nurse flushed the wound. She was using a Toomey syringe, a big 60 cc affair that looked like a turkey-baster and was filled with hydrogen peroxide and saline. She squirted the peroxide liquid into the open wound, the solution filling the hole, then foaming up, before changing into a pale pink fluid that oozed over Jimmy's forearm. Jimmy Ray cried again.

"Shut up, soldier, or I'll sick Mighty Ralph on you."

"No, no, anything but that," Jimmy Ray cried, as Zak pushed him back onto the bed.

Jimmy Ray lay whimpering as the nurse packed the now clean

wound with sterile squares of gauze before wrapping everything in layers of fresh Kerlix dressing. Next, she began unwinding the covering of Jimmy Ray's right leg, where she would repeat the cleansing process.

"Mighty Ralph, oh Mighty Ralph, where are you?" Jimmy Ray cried before he slipped away into semi-consciousness.

"What was that all about?" I asked Lindy later, after we had hung and timed several IVs and mixed a fresh batch to be used by the night shift.

"You'll have to ask Zak," she said, shaking her head.

Two days later I pushed a small stainless-steel cart, fully stocked with sterile gauze, peroxide, and adhesive tape as I followed Bonnie, the dressing nurse, in my first tutorial on how to change dressings in *my* Hell.

Assigned to help Bonnie and me, Zak watched in amused silence as she explained our cruel assignment.

"It's pretty bad," she began, "Most of these guys are so GORKed they have no idea what's happening to them. But the doctors won't order anything for pain for the ones who aren't. The Docs are afraid of making their confusion worse. But damn it, it has to be awful even for the worst patients to be put through dressing changes."

I held the leg of a comatose patient, while Bonnie unwrapped the old gauze. Beneath it lay a 3" x 4" hollow of bright pink flesh, covered by-now dried gauze. Bonnie picked at the corner of the dressing and yanked at the dried, inner layer. The patient barely flinched.

"Why don't you put hydrogen peroxide on the lesion first?" I asked.

"Yes, of course, it would be less painful, but it would also be less effective, and that would defeat the purpose."

"What do you mean?"

"The dried gauze pulls away dead tissue. It helps keep the opened part of the wound clean so it will heal without getting infected. A little bleeding seems to help too."

Beneath the now exposed open area the tissue was bright pink, normal. I listened as Bonnie explained that above all I needed to watch for blackened specks of tissue, yellow or green drainage, or a wound with an especially foul smell.

When I Die I'm Going to HEAVEN

"This looks fine," she said, then gently covered the exposed area with an unfolded 4" x 4" dressing before rewrapping the leg.

We moved on to the next patient. I held his head while Bonnie lifted the last layer of gauze from his skull.

"Oh, this is not good," she said pointing to a beige substance oozing out from this soldier's head wound, which had been sutured closed. "See that, that's brain tissue. He's got some swelling going on here. Probably an infection too."

"Captain, you wanna take a look at this," Bonnie called for Ted.

Ted hurried to the bedside, looked at the skull incision, then quickly flashed a small light into the young man's eyes. "They're sluggish but not fixed, isn't that what we heard in report?" he said, referring to our patient's pupillary response to light.

"I think so," I offered.

"I'll call Jennison," he said, referring to Dr. Derek Jennison, the chief of neurosurgery, who was the physician on call.

By the time we finished rewrapping our patient's head, the medication nurse arrived with a vial of IV mannitol. She popped the vial open, found a port on the patient's IV tubing, stuck the mannitol needle into the port, and began pushing as quickly as she could. When she finished, she opened another vial and repeated the process.

Pushing mannitol was, I would soon learn, hard, messy work. It took effort to push the fluid filled part of the vial into a patient's vein, and, no matter how neat, a nurse simply could not inject the liquid without some of it dripping out. When she finished the front of her uniform was covered with white splotches of dried sugar.

Eventually we reached Jimmy Ray. "Listen up soldier, I have a new 2 L.T. here who thinks she's going to change your dressing." Zak said by way of introduction. Jimmy Ray writhed on the bed, tearing at his dressings.

"We don't think he can see much," Zak informed me.

I reached for Jimmy Ray's hand. "Hi," I said, determined not to let the communication skills I'd learned in college go to waste because I was in a war zone.

"Fuck you."

So much for therapeutic communication, I thought, as I helped

Bonnie unwind Jimmy Ray's head dressing. I was beginning to wonder if I had made a mistake volunteering for Ward 5.

"Where's that Mighty Ralph, I want Mighty Ralph."

"Oh, Ralph's not here. You're going to have to make do with us," Zak announced as he began to remove the dressing from Jimmy Ray's leg.

At lunch, I gathered up my nerve to ask Bonnie an obvious question, "Who is Mighty Ralph?"

Bonnie laughed, then picked up a forkful of her meatloaf, chewing on it thoughtfully, composing her reply.

Finally, she said, "Mighty Ralph Gooyami *is* the spirit on Ward 5."

"Do you mean the spirit *of* Ward 5," I asked, confused.

"Well he may be, but you heard me right. The spirit *on* Ward 5."

"So, you're telling me Ward 5 is possessed?" I asked, laughing.

"Nah, nothing that crazy," Bonnie said, "But then again the rest of the hospital thinks we are crazy, so why not prove it to them?"

"Look," she said, after chewing another forkful of meatloaf. "Zak spent four months in the field before he got here. That he managed to get out of the field and into a safe environment like the 24th Evac is something I think he's very happy about.

"He doesn't talk very much about what it was like to be a medic in a unit constantly on patrol, but I gather that he made up some sort of fairy godfather that protected him from some very bad shit. A lot of other guys might be sending novenas skyward toward St Anthony or whatever, but that's not Zak's style."

"So instead we have Mighty Ralph stead."

"Yup, that would be about right."

"And what exactly is it that Mighty Ralph is supposed to do?" I inquired, still confused. "You know, I've see a lot of strange things happen in this friggin' place. IVs gone dry when they shouldn't, patients die who should have lived, some live who should have died…" She let her meaning hung in the air: Why not blame it all on Mighty Ralph?"

Chapter 5.
MIGHTY RALPH

It was my first day on my own after orientation. In two short weeks I had learned as much about neurosurgical nursing as my compatriots could pour into my brain. Some, like levels of consciousness and pupillary reaction to light were easy to integrate into my understanding of how neurosurgical nursing worked. Others, like changes in pulse, respiration, and temperature were more difficult. Was a fever of 103°F indicative of infection or damage to the hypothalamus? It didn't matter. The one pain reliever we used, usually as a rectal suppository, was Tylenol. To bring down the fever.

Additionally, I had learned what other drugs we used, and when; how to stick a needle in the femoral artery to find out the percentage of oxygen in a patient's blood (this often required saddling the patient's legs to get at his femoral artery), how to use the special cooling "blanket" to bring down temperatures of 104ºF or greater; and how best to reposition patients with spinal cord injuries who could not move themselves.

Jimmy Ray still lay in the bed at the back of the ward, his condition slowly improving.

The days he was more alert outnumbered the days he was lethargic, and he seemed to know where he was. Yet he still had moments where confusion seemed to overwhelm him.

I was medication nurse that day. As I worked, adding the correct amount of sterile water to a vial of dried penicillin, Jimmy Ray began to scream. "Debbie, Debbie Lee May, where are you?"

I put down my syringe and walked over to Jimmy Ray's bed.

"Debbie's not here," I reasoned. "You know that; she's back home in Tennessee, waiting for you." The ER staff had been able to salvage a wallet when they cut his fatigues away from Jimmy Ray's battered body. Inside was a picture of a tall, athletic, sandy haired boy, his arm around a small, thin girl with long, blonde hair. This, apparently, was his girlfriend Debbie.

"Debbie, Debbie, where are you, I need you baby."

"She's not here, Jim. You know that."

"But she *was* here, earlier. I talked to her."

I wondered if Debbie was the person, unseen to us, with whom Jimmy Ray had been chattering away with during some of the morning. He'd seemed a little confused then, but we could easily orient him to time and place by reminding him where he was and what had happened to him.

By then we knew Jimmy Ray could see, though not always clearly. But when he babbled we had no idea what was happening inside his brain. Was he hallucinating or dreaming? Could he differentiate between the imagined and the real? Was this part of Jimmy Ray's healing and thus normal? We had no way of knowing.

I thought there might be another piece to the puzzle. We had a Vietnamese employee, a woman who worked on Ward 5 as both translator and nursing assistant. Her name was Nga but she liked to be called Debbie. Perhaps in his post traumatic fog Jimmy Ray thought Nga, the Vietnamese nursing assistant, was really his girlfriend Debbie. He liked Nga.

"Hello. Jimmy, do you mean Nga? She was just here, helping the nurse change your dressings," I said, trying out my theory.

"Who the fuck is Nga?"

"She's our Vietnamese translator. You know that Jimmy. You were talking to her earlier."

"But that was Debbie."

Zak sidled up to the bed, amused by my attempts to keep Jimmy Ray aware of his surroundings.

"I want Debbie," Jimmy Ray repeated with the determination of an unhappy two year old. Given all he'd been through I wondered if his brain wasn't functioning as that of an unhappy two year old.

I reached for the picture of Debbie Lee May inside Jimmy Ray's bedside stand. But before I could show it to him Zak said, "Listen up soldier, quit screaming or I will sick Mighty Ralph on you."

"Oh, no, not that. Anything but that."

"You know," I said to Zak later, "I had that under control. If you hadn't butt in, he wouldn't had started screaming for Mighty Ralph."

"I know." Zak walked off.

I was pissed. I wanted Jimmy Ray to get better. I thought Zak did too. If so, why had he treated Jimmy Ray so rudely? Had I figured Zak all wrong?

Gathering my courage—for if truth be told, I was a little afraid of the tall corpsman with the bushy moustache—I confronted Zak.

"You know," I began, "I was making progress with Jimmy Ray."

"You only think you were making progress. For all we know Jimmy Ray is going to wind up like some vegetable, shitting in his pants on some neuro-ward in a backwater VA hospital."

"Don't you think we have to try?"

"Hell, yes, Loo-ten-ant," Zak articulated the three syllables of my rank just so, and in doing it, pointed out the naiveté of my view.

"Look," Zak said after we both cooled off, "all this crap about Mighty Ralph and Debbie. It don't mean nothin… I know it, Jimmy Ray knows it, and you ought to learn it."

It don't mean nothin'. I had heard the phrase from the moment I stepped off the plane in Bien Hoa. I was learning exactly what it meant: a way for a young man, who should have been in college or learning a trade, to deal with daily horror of war. *Don't mean nothin'* was a way of coping with the unimaginable, or laughing off the horrible.

Someone as sick as Jimmy Ray get better? *Don't mean nothin'.*

Someone else take a turn for the worse? *Don't mean nothin'.*

Get swept off your feet by a handsome young doctor who, it turns out, has a gorgeous wife and three kids at home? *Don't mean nothin'.*

Fall in love with a chopper pilot who then gets killed? *Don't mean nothin'.*

When you are nineteen, or in my case twenty-two, you had to figure out a way to maintain some inner core of personal strength without letting the unending procession of wounded men your own age or younger, get to you. In a war that most of us, regardless of our personal political views, saw as an unwinnable waste of time, energy, and—most of all—humanity, there had to be a place to shunt our anger and frustration if we were to focus on our duty. We couldn't stop the killing any more than we could stop the war and so *don't mean nothin'* and the creation of Mighty Ralph were as good a way as any to deal with our frustration and anger.

Two nights later I sat listening to report, which began precisely at 1845. My first night shift and I dreaded the idea of having to stay awake for twelve hours. We would work together caring for the patients on 5 and 6, though one nurse usually took responsibility for all of Ward 6 while the another two worked on 5. There were also four corpsmen who shunted between the two wards bathing patients, emptying catheters, changing linen, restocking supplies and scrubbing the floor. It was repetitive, thankless work, but far better than humping a sixty-pound pack through rice paddies and open fields.

We nurses had our own chores: finish whatever dressing changes the day shift had not been able to get to, help the corpsmen, especially with repositioning patients and flipping Stryker frames. And then there was the constant monitoring of patients for changes in mental status or vital signs.

On this, my first night, Zak and his henchman, Howie, a cute young corpsman also from the south side of Chicago, engineered a welcome for me, the new 2 L.T. Around two in the morning, while they bathed and shaved the patients of Ward 5, Zak picked up a container of shaving cream and pointed it at Howie.

"En garde, you asshole," Zak sprayed the shaving cream in Howie's direction. Howie returned fire. Soon foam covered the length of Ward 5. Someone handed me a can of the frothy stuff, and I shot it in their direction.

I had heard about shaving cream battles, a harmless way to blow of steam, cause a laugh or two, be a kid. To an outsider it must have seemed juvenile, and perhaps it was, but I was anxious to play along. The corpsmen still didn't know me very well. I wanted to prove I was one of the guys.

For a few, brief moments we all laughed.

Then Jimmy Ray woke up and began screaming. "Oh God, Oh

God, my head is killing me."

Zak, Howie, the other night nurse and I rushed to his side. "What's wrong Jimmy Ray?" someone asked. But Jimmy Ray did not answer. Instead he lay limply on the bed, unresponsive and pale.

Without a moment's hesitation, I ran to the med room, pulled a big vial of mannitol from the shelf as the other night nurse picked up the phone to call the chief of neurosurgery. Zak and Howie took two sets of vital signs. They were normal.

"Listen to me, Jimmy Ray," Zak began. "Mighty Ralph is right here, he's right over my shoulder and he says you'd better wake up and wake up quick or he's going to be damned pissed at you."

Jimmy Ray did not answer. I popped the top of the big 50 cc container and began pushing the concentrated sugar water into Jimmy Ray's veins as quickly as I could. First one vial, and then a second.

Dr. Jennison plowed through the back door, and strode to Jimmy Ray's bed. He might have given orders for the patient's care over the phone and gone back to sleep. But this was Jimmy Ray. In the time he had been with us he had, in some inexplicable way, come to embody the idiosyncrasies of a ward filled with severely brain damaged patients, watched over by a guardian angel named Mighty Ralph. He belonged to us. He was one of us. And because of that Derek Jennison had as personal a stake as the rest of us in seeing to it that Jimmy Ray got better.

Jennison looked to the charge nurse for report.

"I don't know Major. He was fine one minute, really sleeping like a baby, and then he woke up screaming."

Jennison flickered a light into Jimmy Ray's eyes, which were the same as they had been since the day I arrived: equal and sluggishly reactive to light.

Jennison pinched the skin above Jimmy Ray's right nipple. The young man yelled, then opened his eyes, "What the fuck do you think you're doing?"

Jennison laughed. "I have no more idea what happened than you do. I'm going back to bed. Call me if you need me."

The crisis over, I walked back to the med room, pulled a couple of bottles of D5LR from the fridge and began looking at IVs.

To do so I had to walk past Jimmy Ray. It was impossible to ignore Zak, standing over Jimmy Ray's bed. He spoke quietly, his voice raw with emotion "Don't you ever do that to us again Jim.

"If you do, I *will* sick Mighty Ralph on you."

Chapter 6.
"I'M GONNA GET YOU YET, MIGHTY RALPH"

I stood outside the medication room looking at the hodgepodge of papers pinned to the wall. Most, like mine, were of Snoopy dressed as a World War I flying ace, and all, like mine had been blocked into 365 rectangles, one for each day of our year in Vietnam. We called them DEROS Calendars, which, counting backward, stood for Date of Estimated Rotation Overseas. The day we would go home.

That morning I colored in the rectangle for Day 325. I had been in Vietnam more than a month. It already felt like a year. My sense of time and place were beginning to alter as I worked through one twelve-hour shift after another in a windowless Quonset hut where the lights were kept on twenty-four hours a day.

At least I was no longer the Newbie or the FNG (Fucking New Guy). That honor belonged to 1 LT Carol Ann Rogers, who had arrived on Ward 5 a week after me, and with whom I was developing a friendship so enduring it would last a lifetime.

And yet, Jimmy Ray still lay in his bed at the back of the ward. If I had been on Ward 5 for more than five weeks, Jimmy Ray had been there six. Few patients, no matter how sick, stayed that long. We didn't have the space, and once a soldier's condition was stable he needed to be sent back to the States, where he would receive better care.

To be sure we gave excellent care to the wounded. We were an intensive care unit, after all. But we were not equipped to help our soldiers make the slow progression from the fog of brain trauma to anything resembling normal function. There was no one available to constantly talk to the men, to help them learn to walk, reuse a weakened arm, or recognize the difference between the letters C and G. There was no sister, parent, or friend to be with. Our survivors needed enormous quantities of different but equally important types of intensive therapy. Therapy we were not equipped to provide.

Eventually several of the nurses and corpsmen began to outwardly question Jimmy Ray's continued presence on Ward 5. What was Jennison up to? Why hadn't we shipped him?

Finally, Ted pinned Jennison down. "He is still one sick cookie."

"But don't you think he is stable enough to transfer to Japan?"

"No."

But the evidence was not in Jennison's favor. Jimmy Ray had been on Ward 5 so long his hair was growing back unevenly over his skull incisions. Even most of his frag wounds were healing, scar tissue filling in the opened places on his trunk and extremities.

I was beginning to think that Jennison feared sending Jimmy Ray home because we would miss him. The bond we had created with Jimmy Ray, emblematic in its own twisted way of who we were as *good people*, was so strong many of us secretly wondered what would happen if Jimmy Ray were no longer on the Ward.

Ted wouldn't let the matter drop. "Don't you think he's well enough to be fed?"

"OK," Jennison agreed reluctantly. Zak got some green jello from the kitchen, and spooned a mouthful into Jimmy Ray.

"This stuff tastes like shit." But he ate the entire dishful.

"Maybe we should consider moving him to Ward 6, so he isn't confused by the constant bright lights," I suggested. Ted agreed. All the nurses thought it would help to keep Jimmy Ray oriented to time, if not place, if we moved him to 6, where we turned the lights off at night. The change from light to dark to light again might have been helpful over time but the alteration of his immediate surroundings confused the young soldier. A day after the move, I arrived for duty to discover Jimmy Ray back in his old spot on Ward 5.

"Did he take a turn for the worse?" I asked, alarmed.

"Nah," Howie said. "He couldn't sleep on 6. He asked to move back to 5."

With most of his wounds healed a single nurse could change Jimmy Ray's dressings by herself.

Later one afternoon I set out to clean a few of the remaining open frag wounds on Jimmy Ray's leg for the second time that day. I set up my sterile field, poured saline and peroxide into a stainless-steel bowl, and began unwinding Kerlix from Jimmy Ray's leg, explaining to him that I was about to change his dressing.

Without warning Jimmy Ray roared, "Fuck, you're hurting me." He flung his arms in my direction, kicking and screaming.

"You know this would be a whole lot easier if you didn't fight me," I said after he calmed down a bit.

Jimmy Ray lay with his eyes closed, considering my suggestion. Then he opened one eye, fixed his gaze on me, and said, "Now Lieutenant why would I want to do that?"

Another week passed. Jennison ordered x-rays on Jimmy Ray's fractured arm and leg: they were healed. He ordered physical therapy. The first time a therapist tried to assist Jimmy Ray to a standing position he slumped to the floor, arms and legs weakened by so much time in bed.

"OK," Jennison gave in, "I'm gonna ship him."

In the early morning hours of the day Jimmy Ray was to leave, Zak bathed his patient one last time, dressing him in dark blue hospital pajamas. The two argued the entire time, each invoking Mighty Ralph's name.

In this distillation of the battle between Jimmy Ray and Zak, with a little help from Mighty Ralph, Jimmy Ray got the last laugh. For just as the Air Force corpsmen were about to transfer him from his bed to a stretcher for the bus ride to Bien Hoa Air Force Base he shit his pants. Zak's last act caring for Jimmy Ray was to change his soiled pajamas. Somehow, it seemed fitting, as if Jimmy Ray was proving to us he, too, knew it was time to go home.

Finally, it was time to say goodbye. The night crew stood at the front door of Ward 5, shouting well wishes to this young man whose struggle had become symbolic of our struggle to care for the wounded.

When I Die I'm Going to HEAVEN

As the lead corpsman pushed open the front door, Jimmy Ray sat up on the stretcher, turned round and looked at Zak and the Quonset hut one last time, then shouted, "I'm gonna get you yet Mighty Ralph."

Chapter 7.

BLOWN PUPIL

No one really knew what happened to the little girl. Her parents told the American soldiers standing guard at the entrance to Long Binh Post that she had been struck by a "deuce and a half," one of the ubiquitous two and a half ton trucks that roamed over the Vietnamese landscape where-ever American soldiers went. They knew they did not need to produce the truck, or prove that an American was responsible for their daughter's injuries to gain access to American medical care. It was simply enough to tell someone she had been hurt by an encounter with America's finest.

To the American public, our soldiers may have seemed like a bunch of stoned kids shooting their way through a war they did not start, and certainly did not want to fight. But most were frightened, soft-hearted sons and brothers who could not bear to see a hurt child. So, to the soldiers standing guard that morning it didn't matter what had really happened to her. She was a child caught in a war that had begun before she was born. Of course we would try to save her life.

Major Vincent Antonelli, my favorite of the three neurosurgeons, had admitted her around six in the morning, but had not operated. She was bruised all over, her face swollen, and she was in a light coma. But x-rays showed no skull fracture, no internal injuries.

Antonelli marched onto Ward 5 about ten hundred hours, looking for the team leader.

Me.

"Ward 1 is going to be sending you a new patient in a little bit." He described the child, what he thought might have happened to her, and what he feared.

"I'm really concerned she might have a brain bleed. Any sign her condition is changing I want to know right away."

An hour later I helped the Ward 1 nurse wheel little Bi across the hospital compound and onto the ward. There we transferred her small body to a bed between the nurse's station and the front wall of the medication room.

I listened to report from the Ward 1 nurse: *Antonelli had just left. He was up-to-date on her condition, aware that her level of consciousness seemed ever so slightly deeper.* I took a set of vital signs. Her pulse was fast, but not unusually so. Her respirations were normal. I didn't have a blood pressure cuff small enough for her thin arms, but then blood pressure is not the most helpful vital sign in a child her size. I inspected her bruises, checked the capillary refill on her small foot. Nothing unexpected there.

I flashed a light into her eyes. The right pupil was very slightly dilated, but reacted quickly enough to light. The left pupil *was* dilated: bigger than the right, unable to change much when I flashed the light in her eye. We called Bi's dilated pupil—a sure sign of increasing intracranial pressure—a "blown pupil."

I considered calling Antonelli just to make sure he knew her pupils were uneven in their reaction to light. But the Ward 1 nurse assured me he had just checked her, and we were busy.

Soon after I finished my initial assessment Bi's mother arrived and squatted at the foot of her daughter's bed. Vietnamese family members were always welcome at the 24th Evac. They brought their own provisions, or asked one of our Vietnamese employees to bring them food from a local shop, which they cooked on one burner stoves outside the Ward's back door. They slept under their loved one's bed, assisting the staff with daily care. And they never complained. Not about the unfairness of being caught up in the war, not about sleeping on hard concrete, or of the lights never being turned off. By their standards the air-conditioned ward must have felt frosty. They didn't complain about that either. As foreign as it was to me to see them camping out near their loved one, it was also reassuring. It would be much easier for this little girl if her mother was there when Bi woke up.

I was sure she would.

Twice more that day Antonelli came to check on his patient. He did not bother with a thorough neurological exam, trusting that we would report changes. I started to say something about the blown pupil, but stopped. I thought he knew.

I was learning to live with war's cruelty, dealing as best I could with the ongoing onslaught of pain and death, and my own sense of futility and despair. I knew long before I arrived in Vietnam that the wounded would parade through our doors, like an endless march of doomed souls on their way to Hell. I knew Vietnamese civilians were as much victims of the war as were our men. But I had not thought about the children.

Bi's physical care was routine:
Vital signs every hour √
Assess urinary output every hour √
Check level of consciousness every hour √
Check pupillary reaction to light every hour √
Make sure the IV is running at the proper rate √
Assess skin condition every four hours √
Assist corpsmen with bathing and bed changes √

But there was something about Bi that got to me. She was so small, so innocent looking, lying naked on the rough blue hospital sheets. Her mother looked more resigned than frightened. I wanted to comfort her, too. So, whenever possible, I made a point of giving Bi extra attention. We were already giving her very good care, but I had taken Antonelli's concerns to heart. I wanted this child to survive as much as he did. And so, I bathed the little girl myself, allowing her mother to sit on the bed so she could cradle her in her arms. Bi's vital signs remained normal, her pupils were as they had been from the first time I checked them: unequal and sluggishly reactive to light.

Antonelli and I talked about her at length. Were there any changes? *No.* Then why wasn't she getting any better? *We could not figure it out.*

On the third day, Bi had a seizure. I called Antonelli right away. He ordered some Phenobarbital, then flew onto the unit. I stood by his side while he examined his tiny patient.

"When did she blow the pupil?"
"It was like that when she got here. I thought you knew."
Antonelli shook his head no.
"Shit. She must have blown it when we were transferring her. She must have blown it between here and Ward 1." A distance of no more than twenty yards.
"I'm sorry," I said, fighting back tears. "I started to tell you at least a couple of times."
"Don't beat yourself up. I should have checked her pupils too."
"What are you going to do now?"
"See if I can still save her."

Thirty minutes later Bi was on her way to the OR. Her mother sat quietly as Nga explained what was happening. As we waited for Bi to return her mother squatted where the bed had been, rocking back and forth rhythmically. I wanted to rock with her.

Three hours later Antonelli himself pushed Bi's bed onto the Ward. He looked grim. "She had a big bleed. I'm surprised she's still alive."

"Maybe she'll pull through,' I said, trying to bring hope to a situation that felt as though it had been left behind on that first trip between Wards 1 and 5. If timing was everything the timing of Bi's blown pupil could not have been worse. Fate had already dealt her a cruel injustice. Was there not a bit of good karma left for her?

But Bi did not get better. She continued having seizures. Then she got pneumonia. Every day she seemed to slip further and further away from us.

And then she died.

I was filled with remorse. For my entire nursing career, I was known for giving detailed reports, both verbally and in writing, about the patients in my care. Why then had I not told the doctor about the blown pupil?

Chapter 8.

RIDING IN HELICOPTERS WITH BOYS

"Wanna do something together tomorrow?" Carol Ann asked as we strolled down the walkway toward our hooches after another long shift. The following day, a Sunday, we were both off duty, and I had no plans for the day. I thought I might sleep in, maybe try out the non-denominational Protestant church service at 1030, and then, after lunch, go to the swimming pool across from the Agent Orange dump.

That Long Binh Post had a swimming pool surprised and delighted me. I grew up with a pool and loved nothing more than to spend a Sunday afternoon doing cannonballs or making currents around the edge of the pool with my sisters and friends. But I had mixed feelings about going to the pool across from the 24th Evac. I had been there once, and in my two-piece bathing suit, felt completely exposed, unused to the stares of a hundred or so American men seeing a Round Eyed woman soaking in the water beside them.

And if I went to the pool I would be exposed in another way. Long Binh Post sat on land that had once been jungle. Army bull dozers and Agent Orange had effectively removed almost all the vegetation, and certainly all the trees. This meant the pool was bathtub warm and there was absolutely no shade in which to retreat from the tropical sun. At twenty-two, I had already had more than my fair share of blistering sunburns and didn't want another.

I would have been content to sit in my air-conditioned room and read a book. But I wanted to make friends, and I really liked Carol Ann. She had arrived in Vietnam about a week after me, and had also been assigned to Ward 5. She too had gone to college on an Army scholarship, and wondered what in the hell she was doing in Vietnam. An attractive blonde from Los Angeles, she was more adventurous and outgoing than I.

"What do you have in mind?" I asked.

"Oh, this chopper pilot I know wants to take me to Vung Tau tomorrow. He said I could invite someone to go with me."

"Sure," I said, after a moment's hesitation. We were not supposed to leave Long Binh Post without permission. We were not supposed to take joy rides in helicopters. But Vung Tau was known for its beaches, and I wanted to see something of Vietnam other than the brick dust soil, drab buildings, and dusty roads of Long Binh. I decided to take my chances. What could they do to me if I got caught? Send me to Vietnam?

The next morning Carol Ann and I waited on the edge of the helicopter pad. Although we were off duty, we dressed in fatigues, and carried our regulation purses. But each of us also had a bag filled with towels, shorts, bathing suits, flip flops, sunglasses, cameras, and the like. I also had a book. A voracious reader, I wanted the book with me in case I got bored.

Within moments a Huey (a Bell UH1-H helicopter) gently touched down. Carol's friend Chip jumped from the whirly bird, and dashed up to us.

"Come-on ladies, let's go," he shouted above the chopper's noisy whine. "Your chariot awaits. Just be sure to bend down so you don't get hit in the head by the rotors." He pointed to the helicopter's overhead blades, now zigzagging up and down as the machine idled.

Once inside, Chip introduced us to his co-pilot and the rest of the crew, two of whom manned machine guns affixed to open doors, one on each side of the helicopter. This was a combat-ready flying machine, not one used for dustoff. (By the time I arrived in Vietnam the term "dustoff" was synonymous with unarmed medical evacuation helicopters. Originally coined by an air ambulance pilot, the term "dustoff" referred to the amount of dirt blown into the air by the helicopter's whirling rotor blades.) I didn't know if I felt safer knowing I was protected by two burly sergeants with machine guns, or wished I was in a helicopter with a big red cross painted on its underbelly, and, thus, theoretically off limits to any Viet Cong who might want to take a pot shot at me.

One of the men manning the machine guns handed us headsets so we could hear the chatter among the crew. Someone showed us how to push a control to talk. We were in business.

"Welcome aboard, ladies," Chip spoke over the intercom. "I'm gonna get us high pretty fast so we're out of range of any Gooks looking for an easy target this beautiful Sunday morning. Then we'll find the Mekong and follow it on down to the sea."

One of the door gunners waved Carol Ann and me out of our seats, motioning us to the chopper's open doors so we would have a better look at the landscape. "It's safe, we won't let you fall out," he said, then pointed off to our left. "That's the edge of Saigon over there."

Below, all was a mix of abundant green blending with brown swirls of the river's inlets and eddies. It looked tropically beautiful, yet somehow decayed.

As we flew south toward Vung Tau Carol Ann and I stayed where we were, sitting cross-legged on the floor near the chopper's open doors. Below, the green rushed by. After an hour we saw the first glint of turquoise and then white: The South China Sea and Vung Tau's sandy beaches. Chip brought the helicopter in fast then cut the engine and hopped out.

"Welcome to beautiful Vung Tau."

What had once been a thriving Army Post, complete with hospital, Post Exchange and Officers Clubs was now little more than a collection of shoddy buildings, bunched together inside a perimeter fence.

But there was still the white sand beach, and a bath house of sorts. A few American men cavorted in the warm water, clearly enjoying themselves. Carol Ann and I changed into bathing suits and found our host. Chip had brought something for us to sit on: an olive drab,

100% wool, standard issue Army blanket. He unfolded the blanket with a flourish and placed it on the hot sand before dragging us to the ocean's edge.

We frolicked in the warm water for about an hour, then threw ourselves onto the blanket. It was scratchy, but with our towels neatly resting on top, it was as fine a beach blanket as anything Annette Funicello had ever owned. Chip produced food and cool beer for our makeshift picnic, all the while flirting madly with Carol Ann. She flirted back. The rest of the crew was nowhere to be seen.

Clearly, I was the third wheel. I ran back into the water, cooled off, pulled my book and my sunglasses from my bag, then went in search of shade.

"Is there something wrong?" Carol Ann asked.

"Naw," I said. "It doesn't take much to turn me into a cooked lobster. I need to get out of the sun." Then, finding a place to sit in the shade cast by one of Vung Tau's buildings, I added, "Carry on." I couldn't admit that I had had enough sun and sand and was as bored with the beach as I would have been had I stayed home and gone to the pool.

Eventually, we changed back into fatigues. Chip narrated a short tour of the post. Not much to see except a few buildings housing a few active duty personnel whose job was mostly to look after the beach.

At last the crew assembled and we boarded the 'copter for home. As we headed north Chip banked the helicopter ever so slightly so that Saigon and then the ARVN National Cemetery[*], its rows of headstones positioned in uniformly curved rows, creating an enormous circle of marker after marker, came in view.

The sun was low in the sky when we reached Long Binh. Chip did not take us straight to the hospital. Instead, he showed us Long Binh from the air: the giant Xs created by the intersecting Quonset huts of the 93rd Evac, the forbidding structure of Long Binh Jail—just down the street from us—and finally the 24th Evac.

The hospital, whose enormous size was much more apparent from the air, seemed to glow in the golden light of the setting sun. It wasn't much, but it was home. And I was glad to be back.

After thanking our hosts for a wonderful day away from the war, we dumped our wet bathing suits and towels in our rooms before

heading to the Mess Hall.
> Major Lewis held the door open for us.
> "You girls have a nice time in Vung Tau?" she asked.

---

*Army of Republic of Vietnam

Chapter 9.

SCREAMS IN THE NIGHT

For nurses, there was very little difference between the day and night shifts at the 24th Evac. Patients needed care around the clock, and the wounded arrived at all hours. During any given twelve-hour shift about a third of the nurses and corpsmen were at work, another third were asleep, the rest enjoyed their one day off a week.

The entire post lived under a 2200 hours curfew. But, at the hospital, it was easy to break. No one stood guard at the hospital's entrance counting heads as the clock wound toward 2159. And anyway, there were legitimate reasons why any of us could be out and about well after 10PM: a need to get something from one's room, the excellent midnight breakfasts, a trip to another ward to help during a crisis, or a jeep broken down on the other side of post.

The hospital was protected by two rows of concertina wire and two guard towers, manned from sundown to sunup. But neither made us feel particularly safe. What did comfort us was our location. The 24th Evac was placed well inside Long Binh Post. It would take a very crafty V.C. (Viet Cong,) crossing miles of territory controlled by the United States Army, to get close to the hospital.

Even the constant nightly pounding noise made by "outgoing" mortar shells and rockets being lobbed into the Vietnamese landscape was reassuring—once you got used to the thumping.

For the first time in nine months I felt safe.

When I Die I'm Going to HEAVEN

In July, 1969 I'd been asleep in my room in the Bachelor's Officer Quarters at Fort Sam Houston, Texas, where I and my fellow WRAIN grads were in "Officer Basic Training." Early one Sunday morning I awoke to the sound of the screen door to our building, one floor below, screeching on its hinges. Someone was coming in from a very long night out.

I got up to check on my best friend Joanne, whose room was across the hall. We had been at the same party the previous evening, and when I'd left at 0200 she was still blissfully enjoying the company of a couple of men from our class. The noise I heard had not been made by Joanne. She was asleep in her bed, her door latched only by the safety chain.

For reasons I will never understand I closed my door behind me without locking it, and went back to bed. Twenty minutes later, just as I was drifting off to sleep I was roused to full consciousness by the sensation of the sheet being pulled off my body. Standing at the foot of the bed was a man I had never seen before. I screamed and he ran, the entire incident taking no more than 30 seconds. But I felt as violated as if I had been raped.

In San Francisco, my intended roommate moved in with her boyfriend, leaving me alone in a too large apartment too far away from the city and much too close to where the Zodiac Killer was randomly murdering innocent victims. One night I had a panic attack. I knew exactly what it was, and drove myself to the hospital. Later I saw an Army psychiatrist who assured me I was experiencing a normal response to a frightening situation. He taught me self-hypnosis and assured me I would be fine.

I was better; but I was not fine. The screen door to Hooch 3 squeaking on its hinges whenever someone opened the door sounded eerily like the door at Fort Sam, and I could hear it from my room. The relaxation techniques my San Francisco psychiatrist taught me were helpful, but most nights I lay awake, listening for the door to unexpectedly screech long after I'd turned off the light. How could I learn to ignore it, when nine months earlier that very same noise had heralded my attacker sneaking into the Bachelor Officer's Quarters?

Today my behavior would be considered classic symptoms of

PTSD, but in 1970 no one recognized PTSD, or its signs. Even the few people who understood severe psychological damage could result from traumatic events thought it took combat, or at the very least penetration, to elicit a response like mine.

A Red Cross volunteer named Kathleen lived across the hall from me. There was very little contact between most of the nurses and the "Donut Dollies." Sadly, most nurses, overwhelmed by how sick our patients were, didn't appreciate what the Red Cross Workers did. So, I had made no effort to get to know Kathleen. She seemed pleasant enough, but I thought her job was cushy. I did not see her as another woman dealing with, or helping others cope with the horror of war. Perhaps, over time, we would have become friends. Who knows? Circumstances never gave us the chance.

One night about six weeks into my tour, I come back to my room after report, took a shower, put on pajamas and sat on my bed, reading a book. I didn't drink very often, and hated the feeling of being on display that accompanied being at the Officer's Club without a companion. And anyway, I was usually too tired.

On this particular night, I kept my door open until bedtime, reading a book, and welcoming anyone who wanted to chat. No one did. Kathleen and I said polite hellos, shared a few mundane comments about our day. At 2300 hours I turned off the light and locked myself in my room for the night.

As usual, I had trouble falling asleep. A little after midnight I had just begun to doze off when Kathleen's terrified screams pierced the quiet, wrenching me into full consciousness. I knew that scream. Kathleen was in real trouble.

As I, and several of my fellow nurses, rushed to her aid, her door flew open. A tall, muscular man charged past me and out the front door. My attacker had never been caught. I was not about to let the same thing happen to Kathleen. I ran after the man in my bare feet.

One of the nurses in my hooch was engaged to an infantry officer who, against regulations, spent the night with her whenever he could get to Long Binh. He was there that night, though I hadn't known it when I gave chase. Seconds later the fiancé sprinted past me in hot pursuit of Kathleen's attacker. I stopped running and returned to the hooch.

Kathleen sat crying on her bed. Between sobs she told how she had gotten up to use the bathroom, and when she did, her attacker entered her room. In the five minutes she'd been gone he had put the head of her bed on blocks and rigged the headboard with a rather elaborate set of ropes. Kathleen was just noticing that her light was inexplicably turned off when the man jumped her from behind. She had just enough time to scream before he attempted to cover her mouth with duct tape. When we came to her rescue we saved her from being raped, or worse.

Twenty minutes later the fiancé returned with Major Kelly, who was supervisor that night. They had caught the perpetrator! Knowing he was being pursued Kathleen's attacker had veered off the covered walkway and was running along the back of the surgical wards, and fell into a drainage ditch behind Ward 1. A nurse happened to be standing at the back door, copping a cigarette. A rather burly woman, she lifted the assailant to his feet, smelled alcohol on his breath and saw the drug induced dilation of his pupils.

Enclosing him in a strong wrestler's hold, she was in the process of insisting he be seen in the Emergency Room when the fiancé rushed onto the scene. Armed with the knowledge that this man needed to be detained and arrested for attempted rape the two dragged him into the ER. Someone called the MPs.

Reluctantly Kathleen allowed Major Kelly to escort her to the ER for examination. There was only one empty stretcher and it was next to her attacker. When Kathleen saw him she screamed again. Someone put a privacy screen around her. As soon as they were able the MPs took her attacker away. Eventually, he was locked up in "LBJ": Long Binh Jail, a military prison within walking distance of the hospital.

By then word of the assault raced through the remaining nurses' quarters. Women from all four buildings milled around the entry to our hooch. Not unkindly, Major Kelly shooed people back to bed. Knowing he could be punished no matter how bravely he had come to Kathleen's defense she suggested the fiancé might want to leave before his presence was officially noted. To a woman we protested.

We felt safer knowing there was a man sleeping nearby. Married to a senior non-commissioned officer, Major Kelly knew something about breaking Army regulations. She relented, but suggested, our gallant protector might want to leave very early the next morning.

Someone sent word from the ER that they had given Kathleen some IV valium and put her to bed in one of the "private rooms" on Ward 6. The crisis was over. We went back to our beds, but not to sleep.

Emotions ran high after the attack. We had always felt safe from the Viet Cong; what about our own men?

LTC LeBlanc's first response after hearing of the night's activities was to declare she would build yet another guardhouse, then envelope the four hooches in more concertina wire to guard her nurses. The 2200 curfew would be more strictly enforced. There would be no more late night rendezvouses, no matter the quality of the relationship. She didn't care that several of the junior nurses were married or engaged to men who spent weeks in the boonies. No more turning a blind eye whenever husbands or boyfriends got a brief respite to be with their beloveds.

"They'll be more than one LBJ on this road when I'm done," she threatened. Fearful that what little freedom we had would be taken from us we protested.

"Let some male officers move in with us," we countered. Quarters filled with officers of both genders would easily solve the problem, and we would feel safe. LTC LeBlanc softened her position, but still wanted more protection for her nurses. Eventually the furor died down, the guardhouse not built until long after I returned home.

Devastated by the attack, Kathleen asked the Red Cross to send her home. Without her testimony, there could be no conviction. Her assailant went free.

The events of that night worsened my own sense of vulnerability. The following afternoon I dug through the mess hall's discarded containers until I found an empty three-pound coffee can. For the rest of my stay in Vietnam I peed into a can if I awoke during the night.

Valium was not a controlled drug in 1970 and we kept huge stock bottles of it on Ward 5.

I filched a near empty bottle, and for the rest of the year, on the nights I couldn't sleep I self-medicated with valium.

When I returned home people asked me if I had been in much danger during the war.

Usually I told them that the mere size of Long Binh separated me from the Viet Cong. It was too complicated to tell them I felt safe from the enemy but not from our own men.

Chapter 10.
JOANNIE

The heat of an early tropical evening hit me full force as I stepped out of my hooch on my way to an early dinner, and then to the start of another twelve-hour night shift. Hearing someone shout my name, I peered down the long walkway and saw Joanne, still wearing her green dress uniform, dragging a suitcase and duffel bag behind her.

"Joannie," I cried, my heart leaping with joy. Whatever the rest of the year brought I could handle it. My best friend from the world was here. With her for company I could survive anything.

"You made it," I said, holding her close. "You look different," she replied.

I did not want to tell her I was already tired of being surrounded by the wounded or the dying. She would find out soon enough. Instead, I focused on my hair, which I was forever trying to grow long, only to get it cut short once again.

"What you don't like my stylish outfit—or my hair?" I joked. Not knowing where I would be going, or if there would be anyone but a barber to cut my hair, I had it cut into the shortest pixie possible before I left home. I was already starting to grow it out.

I was dressed for work in jungle fatigues and combat boots, standard outfit for the year. A pack of cigarettes was tucked into my left shirt sleeve pocket along with a lighter, bandage scissors, a small flashlight and a pen. I had a twelve-inch length of unused Penrose drain—stretchy rubber tubing—wrapped around an epaulet in case I needed to draw blood or start an IV. A Kelly Clamp was snapped onto the epaulet as well. I occasionally had to clamp an IV with it, but mostly I used it to open the metal covering of dried penicillin vials.

Like most of my fellow nurses I used even more tubing to "blouse" my pant legs just at the top of my combat boots. I liked the look, it was just a bit cooler, and eventually blousing one's pant legs would become a kind of symbol of rebellion among the junior nurses. But I didn't care about any of that then. I was just glad to see Joanne.

Our friendship had been forged during the two years we'd spent at Walter Reed, especially during our psychiatric nursing rotation and later when we were assigned to the same clinical group for community health nursing. We had visited each other's homes, studied for State Boards together, and had driven in tandem to Fort Sam Houston with another WRAIN Grad. I loved her like a sister, and if someone had asked me to choose a classmate to go Vietnam with me I would have chosen Joanne.

"Do you know your assignment, what hooch are you in?"

"I'm going to the ICU, of course." Joanne had just completed a six-month training course in intensive care nursing.

Then she added, "I think I'm in hooch four."

"Well, yeah, there's an empty room in four, but I'm next door in three. There is someone from three DEROSing in the next couple of days. When you see COL LeBlanc tomorrow ask to move into our hooch when that room opens up. We have a great bunch of people." I went on to explain that one of our classmates from Walter Reed was in the room next to mine.

Joanne was stunned by the colossal amount of information I expected her to absorb instantaneously.

"Look," I added, "I've got to be at work in about 45 minutes, let's go get something to eat. The food here is better than at Walter Reed."

An hour later I reported for duty, listening to the evening's litany of injuries, the progress and set backs of the day. Ward 5 was uncharacteristically quiet, it would be a relatively easy night. As the charge nurse doled out assignments I asked what must have seemed like a ridiculous question: "Do you guys think you could do without me for an hour or so. My best friend from the world just got here and I'd like to spend some time with her."

Someone laughed, then Ted shooed me away with a wave of his hand. "Be back before your gown turns into rags," someone else joked.

One good thing about Ward 5: we looked out for each other. With our reputation as the worst place in the hospital in which to work, we nurtured our friendships. In today's terms, *we had each other's back.*

Always aware of the thin line between being our leader and our superior, Ted fostered our sense of pride, and with it our respect for him as our Head Nurse. He had a knack for achieving just the right balance of discipline, independence, and respect. In less than two months I had come to admire his leadership. On this night, it meant sending one of his junior officers off the Ward for a couple of hours so she could welcome her best friend to the war.

I found Joanne unpacking underwear and tee shirts. The room in Hooch 4 to which she had been assigned was much like mine: drab and uninteresting. None of its previous occupants had tried to fix it up with colorful paint, an armchair, or the trappings of life back in the world. I was working on mine, even if I couldn't quite decide what color I wanted the walls. At least I had a coverlet, hand quilted in a double wedding ring pattern by my grandmother. Most of the pieces had come from dresses my mothers had made for my sisters and me as children. It reminded me of home.

"Look," I said again, "you got to move into three. There are really good people there. There's a terrific room at the back end of the hooch. You should ask to move there before anyone else decides they want it."

Joanne surveyed the dingy room. "What makes that room better?" she asked. "It's in the same hooch with me."

"Some people have really decorated their rooms. The one you would be going into in 3 is very nice. It's got some built in shelves and some other nice touches." I went on to describe some of the ways my fellow nurses had turned their rooms into fantastic living spaces. Among the best was the room with its burgundy wall paper, across the hall from me. Everyone wanted that room, and Doreen, who I'd met on my very first night in country had already claimed it.

"What about being in the back of the hooch?" Joanne asked.

"I don't think it's a problem. If you want to sneak somebody in after curfew, it might be easier from the back than the front." We both laughed.

Then I pointed to the gold band on her left ring finger. "What's that for?"

"Somebody told me I should wear a wedding ring to reduce the number of times guys hit on me."

I laughed. With a full lipped smile, straight white teeth, curly brown hair, and a pert figure, Joanne was a living poster of the all-American girl. "Trust me the ring won't keep you from getting hit on. And there are plenty of nice single guys here. If you meet the right guy you would have some explainin' to do, Lucy." I said, parodying Ricky Ricardo's questions about Lucy's escapades.

"That's not likely to happen."

I laughed again. "You never know. You can always create a serious boyfriend back in the world if you need to."

She removed the ring and threw it in her dresser drawer. "What about you Hessel? You dating anybody?"

"Naw, I haven't met anyone that interesting. Most of the doctors—the really nice ones, anyway—are married. But there are a lot of helicopter pilots. It's mostly a matter of timing, or wanting to meet somebody. So far I haven't cared."

"What do you do when you're not working?"

"Believe it or not there's a swimming pool across the street. The water's like bath water, but it is a distraction." I described my jaunt with Carol Ann to Vung Tau, the times I had hitched hiked to PXs away from the 24th Evac just for a change of scenery, and of visiting our mutual friend Carolyn, who was at the 93rd Evac.

"There are movies in the middle of the compound for everyone a couple of nights a week.

"And there are movies in the O Club. You can buy a rum and coke for 50¢. Sometimes I'll go to the club for an hour or so after work. But you know me; I'd just as soon stay home and read a book than go to the O Club. I feel too much like I'm on display.

"Most of the doctors are married, and that's an involvement I don't want. According to my friend Carol Ann, they call relationships between single nurses and married doctors 'Vietnam Marriages', and that is something I don't want.

"Trust me. There are endless opportunities to meet guys," I added, looking at my watch. "Look," I said, "I've got to go to work. And I bet you're tired. I'll see you tomorrow."

I practically skipped down the long walkway to Ward 5. I knew Joanne and I would not spend every off-duty moment together, we would both make other friends in Vietnam. It was simply sufficient to know she was there.

Chapter 11.
WHEN I DIE I'M GOING TO HEAVEN... BECAUSE THIS IS HELL

Doreen, who took over the burgundy wall papered room when Sandy went home, had friends who worked in supply. One afternoon I came down to the hooch after lunch to discover a large stack of wooden crates standing outside Doreen's door. Inside two handsome young men worked diligently to tear the crates into individual wooden slats.

"Hey, guys what're you doing?" I asked, stepping over the crates so I could enter my room. I had heard about Doreen's plans for the room, but didn't understand how wooden crates could be involved. But as the day progressed I could see what was happening: Doreen's friends were turning her cot into an elevated platform bed. Below it she would have room for a comfortable chair or a couch and a table.

Their craftsmanship was obvious and Doreen burst with pride as the men turned her room into a thing of beauty. It was the envy of every nurse living in the junior female officers' quarters.

I considered asking the men to scrounge some packing crates for me, but Doreen herself was getting short and I had been there long enough to know I could commandeer her room when she went home. I was tempted because my adventures in interior decorating clearly indicated I'd better stay a nurse. When I painted my room I had wanted my walls to be a sandy sort of mauve; instead they

When I Die I'm Going to HEAVEN

*When I painted my room I hoped for a dusty mauve,
but it looked more like poop.*

had turned out the color of peanut butter. Or another soft squishy substance with which we were all too familiar.

Then, Doreen discovered a major problem with her newly created living space: cockroaches. For some reason, the pesky insects seemed drawn to the wood in her room. Roaches and other insects were everywhere, but they seemed to especially like Doreen's room.

I decided to stick with my brown painted walls and the posters I'd put up for additional decoration. I'd found a piece of unused carpeting, and placed it beside my bed. I also had a small bookshelf which I'd adorned with a doll my youngest sister Susie, who was only fourteen, had bought with her meager savings, to give me as a farewell present. And I had a red-painted plaster Buddha—a "gift" from the room's previous occupant. My decorations were minimal and I decided I liked it that way. With the hand sewn double wedding ring quilt from my grandmother on my bed, and the posters on my walls, the room seemed to fit me.

I also had scrounged a small night stand to hold my current book and a bottle of crème de menthe, my soporific of choice after a long night shift. I liked sitting in bed reading whatever came my way until the combination of work related fatigue, a big breakfast, and a couple of ounces of the sweet green liquid told me I could drift off until it was time to get up around 1700, then begin the process all over again.

Eventually I would purchase a small refrigerator and hotplate from a nurse whose tour was over. But I rarely used them. Most of the time I was content to eat whatever the mess hall had to offer.

When the room at the back of Hooch 3 became available Joanne moved in. Her new space held some creative touches of its own, including custom made shelves, fashioned from the ever-popular packing crates. There was just enough wood to give Joanne her own, albeit less invasive, problems with roaches. But she liked her living space and stayed there throughout her time in Vietnam. Being near the backdoor turned out to be a bonus: eventually Joanne *would* have a man to sneak into the Hooch.

We tearfully said our good-byes to Doreen when her time in-country ended. But it wasn't long before a new nurse arrived to take over the roach room. Her name was Stephanie and she was assigned to work along-side Joanne on Ward 2. Like the rest of us, she had gone to nursing school on an Army scholarship. Stephanie was from Louisiana and it showed every time she opened her mouth.

A beautiful young woman with long brown hair pulled back in a ponytail Stephanie was so self-conscious about the way her fatigue blouses hid what little cleavage she had, she decided to order a bust developer from an advertisement she'd seen in a woman's magazine. It took forever for the two physical therapy quality stretch bands to arrive with instructions on how to do chest presses and flies. The creator of this mail-order scam insisted the equipment worked better if the user repeated the chant "I must, I must, I must develop my bust" while exercising.

We laughed at the absurdity of Stephanie walking up and down the hooch doing flies, repeating "I must, I must, I must develop my bust," but absolutely understood the reasoning behind her attempt at natural breast enhancement. By the end of a shift we could be covered in blood and dirt. (Our patients usually arrived at the 24th Evac filthy from being on patrol.) Dressed in combat boots and

When I Die I'm Going to HEAVEN

Relaxing in Susan's room while Stephanie reads about bust enhancement. We're hanging out together in Susan's psychedelic room. I am the one wearing glasses while writing home.

fatigues we looked like one of the guys. That didn't mean we had to *look* like them. I didn't have to worry about bust enhancement, and my combat boots were comfortable. I fought back by growing out my hair, frosting it, and wearing enough Youth Dew the odor could herald my arrival at 20 paces.

Soon after Stephanie arrived our Hooch welcomed yet another Newbie into the group.

Born and raised in the St Louis area, Susan had actually joined the Army after becoming disenchanted with civilian nursing. This made her a bit of a maverick in our eyes, a perception enhanced when she fought—and won—the right to be the only female nurse ever to be assigned to the POW ward. When it closed she moved to orthopedics, where she spent the remainder of her tour. Susan's room, in the middle of the hooch was painted a psychedelic marine blue and hot pink. Because of its location it often became the gathering place for the four of us.

Because she had gone to Officer's Basic with them, Susan knew just about every Dustoff and Med-Evac pilot in our part of Vietnam. One of them was a handsome young Lieutenant named Jim Kautz, stationed at the 45th Medical Company, Air Ambulance, or simply "45th Dustoff," located on the grounds of the 93rd Evac. On any given night, Susan seemed to know where there was a party of helicopter pilots. Once she insisted I accompany her to a party at 45th Dustoff, but I chickened out at the last minute. I've often wondered what would have happened if I'd met the man to whom I have been married for forty-five years in Vietnam, a pilot with 45th Dustoff, rather than after we both came home.

At the same time Susan had a budding relationship with a chopper pilot who flew combat missions. When he was wounded he became her patient on Ward 9. Her fervent pleas to be send to Japan with him as a "private duty nurse" fell on deaf ears. Since they were neither married nor engaged the Army brass had no interest in fulfilling her request.

Stephanie had an on again, off again relationship with a First Cavalry Air Mobile (First Cav) Med-Evac pilot, and was pursued by several of the doctors.

I could have dated as much as I wanted but I was still recovering

L to R: Susan, Joanne, & Stephanie in Hooch #3.

from a broken engagement during my final months of college. Near the end of my time in Vietnam I finally loosened up and began dating, but it did not end well, either. Better to stay home and read a book.

Among our hooch-mates were two nurses who were in Vietnam because of the men in their lives. My classmate Lynn, whose room was next to mine, would eventually become engaged to an infantry officer who visited whenever he could. Valerie was married to a man whose job was so secret we thought he was probably assigned to Army Intelligence. If he wasn't, he certainly had no interest in disabusing us of this impression. When he got the chance to visit Val he seemed to abruptly appear and then just as quickly disappear. He wore fatigues that seemed to be missing all identifiers but his Captain's bars and his name. Could he have been in the CIA?

Carol, who lived in 4, had grown up about 10 miles from me and graduated from an arch-rival high school. Like me she had applied to join the WRAIN program, but had not been accepted. Instead she went to a local hospital school of nursing, and from there into the Army. At her first duty assignment she'd met her husband-to-be, a Special Forces helicopter pilot attached to the First Cav. Strikingly handsome with a well-groomed handlebar mustache, Larry liked to show up at odd times, too. But his visits did not have the same degree of stealth Val's husband's did. When Larry was around we all knew it. His was a larger than life personality and because of his Special Forces training he was used to eating whatever was available. He delighted in picking up stray insects from the floor or walls of our hooch, turning them into a snack, so he could show off.

Once he ate an insect he—decades later—confessed left a bad taste in his mouth for three weeks.

Another resident of Hooch 3 was another Lieutenant, Liz Wilson, who would be assigned to Ft Knox, KY with Carol Ann and me after Vietnam.

One evening, Susan, Joanne, Stephanie and I gathered in Susan's room, writing letters home and making bad jokes about everything from being in Vietnam, to whether I should go after a particularly cute corpsman I really liked.

"Hey, Liz, want some help with that care package?" one of us asked offhandedly as Liz walked by, her arms laden with a large box from home.

"You're gonna love this one," she said, proffering a *Hagar the Horrible* cartoon. It showed Hagar's wife in some silly situation. The punch line was a question: "Did your mother wear combat boots?"

This struck us as particularly funny. Most of us hoped someday we would be able to tell our children their mother had indeed worn combat boots.

Liz, who worked on Ward 15, the maxillo-facial unit, looked especially exhausted that evening.

"How are you?" Someone asked.

"I hate this fucking war." Liz, who rarely swore, plopped herself onto a space on the floor.

We commiserated for a while, then Liz stood, ready to return to her room. Turning to us she uttered, "When I die I'm going to Heaven, because this is Hell."

Chapter 12.
CAMBODIA

In April 1970 there were approximately 400,000 American soldiers on the ground in Vietnam. About 50,000 were Marines. The rest were Army. This number does not include Navy forces patrolling the Mekong River, or the Vietnamese coast. Nor does it include Air Force Personnel either in Vietnam, Okinawa, or Guam, many of whom were attached to B-52 squadrons dropping thousands of pounds of bombs on the Vietnamese landscape.

On 20 April, just days after Apollo 13 returned home safely, President Nixon announced a troop reduction of 150,000 men by the end of the year. But as spring turned toward summer back home—or, in ours case the rainy season—it was clear military planners had something else in mind. Yes, there would be a drawndown of 150,000 slots to be filled by American soldiers. But in the meantime, President Nixon decided to take advantage of a series of unexpected events.

For years, we had had an edgy but workable bond with the Vietnamese government.

Nearby Cambodia was officially a neutral country, but in many ways, it was already controlled by the North Vietnamese. Many ethnic Vietnamese lived in the eastern most part of Cambodia, what some cartographers called "The Parrot's Beak." In addition to Cambodian and ethnic Vietnamese civilians, the Parrot's Beak was home to about 40,000 North Vietnamese and Viet Cong.

Early in 1970 many ethnic Vietnamese living in Cambodia were massacred by Cambodian Communists—the notorious Kmer

When I Die I'm Going to HEAVEN

Triage. The pilot, visible at the front of the helicopter, is 1LT James Kautz

Rouge. The South Vietnamese Government sent ARVN soldiers into Cambodia hoping to save their countrymen. Without success.

Meanwhile Cambodia's leader, Prince Sihanouk, went to Paris to "take the cure," and while he was there General Lon Nol overthrew the government, replacing it with one more friendly to both South Vietnam and the United States.

Seeing this as an excellent opportunity to eradicate both Viet Cong and North Vietnamese Army troops President Nixon ordered senior Pentagon officials to develop a plan for the invasion of Cambodia. It would not be an extension of a war from which we were trying to extricate ourselves, but rather an action designed to push the enemy further north and west, away from South Vietnam.

We learned about The Cambodian Incursion the same way most Americans did: on the radio. In our case, someone notified us to turn on AFVN Radio (Armed Forces Viet Nam Radio) to listen to a special broadcast of messages from both Nixon and the MACV Commander Creighton Abrams.

Moments before Ted turned up the volume on his small portable radio we joked that perhaps we were going home. The news we had

Helicopter arriving with the wounded

invaded Cambodia surprised and stunned us, but we were not nearly as upset as were the thousands of Americans who protested at places like Kent State.

The enemy had no respect for national borders, why should we? Moreover, many of us felt that wiping out a significant number of North Vietnamese Regulars and Viet Cong would hasten our government's ability to get us home.

A mood of uneasy anticipation settled over the hospital. The 12th Evacuation Hospital in Cu Chi and the 93rd and 24th Evacuation Hospitals in Long Binh were the hospitals closest to the "Parrot's Beak." We expected an influx of patients, and, after a few days we were not disappointed.

Once the wounded began arriving we were busy, busier than we had been before May 1970, and busier than we would be afterward. The whump, whump of helicopter rotors filled the air day and night. Surgical teams worked long hours and everyone stayed beyond their twelve hour shifts if needed. Sometimes, when the sounds of helicopter landings seemed unending we would wander over to the Emergency Room or Ward 1 to offer an extra set of hands.

When I Die I'm Going to HEAVEN

Fire Base Mace

The atmosphere inside was one of controlled chaos. The offers were appreciated, but, for the most part the best thing we could do was stay out of the way.

Afterward, for about a month, the hospital was quiet. We had more empty beds on Ward 5 than we'd ever had. We thought we might be able to have two days off a week, or perhaps work eight-hour shifts. But the Army, in its infinite wisdom, made different plans. Rumors began flying that the 12th Evac in Cu Chi would close before year's end. That would leave the 93rd and 24th Evacs, and the 3rd Field Hospital in Saigon as the three remaining hospitals in the southern-most part of South Vietnam.

It gave us an uneasy feeling to know the lights were slowly being shut off, but we were still in Vietnam, still tending to the wounded. I have yet to read a judgment about the success of the Cambodian Incursion. I only know it was the most difficult and exhausting month of my life.

When the census—and thus the hospital's daily pace—returned to normal we did seem to have a little more breathing space. But the War somehow seemed to find a way to fill it. Before long we were busy as usual.

Chapter 13.
BRUNHILDA ALERTS

Eventually both COL Leo and his wife, COL Lillian LeBlanc were ready for their return to the United States. After duly bidding them farewell at a traditional "hail and farewell," we welcomed our new C/O, COL Charles, "Charlie," Cochrane, MD, and our new Chief Nurse, LTC Hildegarde Wangerstein.

COL Cochrane was as good a commanding officer as they get, much loved by the people who served under him. He earned the respect of both career officers and doctors who had been drafted, often during the last months of their residency program, by setting a good example: he was organized, compassionate and fair. Many people kept in touch with him after Vietnam, and mourned his death in 2006, when he died at 85. Looking at his Online obituary I can still see, in his withered face, the man who guided the hospital through the ensuing 12 months.

I knew LTC Wangerstein from my six months at Letterman where she had taught surgical nursing, and I worked in the recovery room next door. LTC Wangerstein seemed like a nice person, but I didn't know her that well. What I did know was that she was hard of hearing and at Letterman had undergone surgery to repair her stapes, one of the ear's small bones. She had even published an article, in a premier nursing journal, about her experience with the surgery.

Within a few weeks of her arrival it became eminently clear that as far as the junior officers were concerned Hildegarde Wangerstein did not know how to manage a 350-bed hospital in a war zone. The constantly changing needs of a constantly changing patient population seemed beyond her ability to grasp. Personal problems among the nurses? She seemed incapable of handling those as well. Over time, the two Assistant Chief Nurses, "the two Pegs," but especially MAJ Margaret Lewis, took over the most important parts of managing the day to day functioning of the hospital. We didn't dislike LTC Wangerstein so much as we held her in disdain. She always seemed to be worried about the wrong thing.

Florence Nightingale had established nursing, and became a heroine to the British people during the Crimean War, because of her simple tenants of clean air, clean food, and clean bodies. Thousands of men had lived because Nightingale had insisted they be bathed daily, and their sheets be changed at regular intervals. Thus, paying attention to a patient's hygiene needs was, and still is, a particularly important aspect of good nursing care.

LTC Wangerstein, who we started calling Colonel Brunhilda behind her back, must have been channeling old Flo because she paid an inordinate amount of attention to patient hygiene, rather than all aspects of keeping our wounded men alive.

One of LTC Wangerstein's favorite daily activities was to make rounds on all the wards, and rightfully so. But she did not inspect the IVs to see if they were running on time, did not look to see if a dressing was soaked with blood. She rarely asked the head nurse if the patient care load was manageable or if we needed help.

What she did was look at fingernails. I happened to be standing near her, changing an IV bottle when I learned first-hand of the Colonel's fingernail fascination.

"Lieutenant, could you come here please?"

"Yes ma'am."

"Why isn't this patient washed?" she asked, lifting his limp hand, its fingernails still encrusted with the ochre colored dirt that was Vietnam.

"I believe he has been bathed," I replied. "Usually the corpsmen on Ward 1 wash new patients before they send them to us." I lifted the sheet covering the man in question and could see that his skin was clean, his face shaved.

"Well, you need to get a nail brush and some cuticle sticks and get that dirt out from under his nails."

"I'm in charge of wound care today," I replied, trying to keep my cool. Did she not know I cared a lot more about the man's brain than his fingers?

"That is an order Lieutenant."

I would gladly have followed the Colonel's directive if I wasn't up to elbows in open wounds, some of which might be infected.

I didn't even know if we had nail brushes or cuticle sticks on the ward. Since graduating from nursing school I hadn't given that many bed baths. The Army's unwritten policy was whenever possible male patients deserved male nursing assistants to help with their hygiene needs. (The same held true for inserting catheters. In my entire career as a nurse I only once placed a catheter into a male patient's bladder—under the supervision of one of *my* nursing students who had been a corpsman in the Army!)

Looking to Ted for reinforcements, I got a smile. He thought it was funny! Brunhilda stomped off the ward, warning me she would be back.

"Don't let her bother you. Her bark is worse than her bite," Ted advised.

An hour later I found LTC Brunhilda at the patient's bedside with a pan of soapy water, a nail brush, and cuticle sticks. I fervently hoped she was learning just how much the brick red dust of Vietnam got into every orifice—and under one's nails.

The most significant contact we junior nurses would have with Colonel Brunhilda began in the most innocuous fashion. Everyone arriving in Vietnam was issued standard Army apparel. In our case that meant jungle fatigues, cotton tee shirts the nurses rarely wore, a floppy ("boonies") hat, canvas topped combat boots, and olive drab wool socks. Wool "breathes" better than cotton, and so was much more practical for men on patrol who needed to keep their feet dry.

Most of has been told to bring our own, neutral colored, cotton knee socks from home. As the year progressed we asked our families to send more socks, still in neutral colors. Then one day someone in Hooch 4 received a pair of argyle socks in a care package.

The next day she wore them with her bloused fatigue pants, so that one could see her socks sticking out between the top of her boot and the bottom on her pants. We loved the way she looked. Pretty soon we were writing home, asking our parents to send us the most outrageously patterned socks they could find. We gave nurses going to Hong Kong or Sydney on R&R (a week's vacation for "rest and relaxation") extra cash to bring back crazily patterned socks. And they did.

At first Colonel Brunhilda tried to ignore this minor but ever-growing infraction. She spoke to us individually. She called a meeting. Or had Peg Lewis call one. *The wild socks under bloused fatigue pants would no longer be tolerated.*

Most of us ignored the directive. A few days later LTC Wangerstein called for an inspection at 0645. Unheard of! Nurses beginning the day shift were expected to line up along the Ward 5 side of the hospital to see if we were properly in uniform. Nurses not on duty were expected to show up, too.

We made sure our boots were polished, our uniforms ironed, and our pants correctly bloused. To a woman each one of us wore some sort of wildly colored socks. Brunhilda started to give us a lecture about respecting military decorum, then stopped. Exasperated, she turned on her heel and headed for her office. LTC 0/ LTs and CPTs 1. After all, what could she do? Send us to Vietnam?

Eventually Joanne and Stephanie would become involved with two helicopter pilots from the First Cavalry's Medical Evacuation unit at Fire Base Mace. Because their mission was to bring patients to the 24th Evac they had a habit of swooping in to visit whenever they could.

One day, after listening to our usual litany of complaints about the Colonel one of the guys declared what Brunhilda really needed was to get laid. They jokingly plotted about how they could make this happen. Each, in turn, offered or refused his service to our cause, laughing as only a testosterone driven twenty-five-year-old male could laugh.

But the idea of Brunhilda alerts simply would not die. By then Joanne and her beloved, Monty, were deeply involved in a relationship that ended in marriage. (One that is still going strong after forty-six years.) Hearing of someone's distress about Brunhilda prompted the pilots to take to the airwaves. Pilots flying into the 24th Evac would be told they were on Brunhilda alert. Nothing happened because of it. There was nothing that could be done. We were already in Vietnam.

Chapter 14.

THE DINNER PARTY

A few months after she arrived in Vietnam, Joanne decided we needed to have a dinner party.

"You want to have what?" I asked, amazed.

"You know, Hessel," she said, using my college nickname, "a party with food, where we sit down and enjoy each other's company and pretend we are leading normal lives."

"And how exactly do you plan to pull off that feat?" I meant the dinner party, but I wondered if anything short of a plane ticket home would make any of us feel as though we were leading normal lives.

And yet we did have a sort of norm. At work, we were professionals, concentrating on saving lives. Every nurse and corpsman I knew did her or his best to give outstanding patient care. Doctors and nurses tangled when questions about patient care arose. Yet, we could usually see beyond this, making friendships within a loose and ever evolving coterie of surgeons, nurses, and Medical Service Corps officers. In each other's company, we could let down our guard and simply be. Then we were women first and nurses second. The men checked their medical credentials at the door. Off duty we could be outrageous or silly, anything but clinical or analytical. A dinner party would be a fine way to honor how our connectivity strengthened us.

In the hands of a lesser woman the dinner party would have been a logistical nightmare.

But this was Joanne, the "honors graduate" of WRAIN '69 and the same person, who, a few weeks later, would take care of a Vietnamese child, hiding him under the noses of the hospital's commanders, while his father recuperated from catastrophic injuries.

"What do you have in mind?" I asked, shaking with laughter at the mere concept of us preparing, cooking for, and serving dinner to 18 or 20 people while going about our daily duties.

"I'd love steak, but we don't have a grill, and anyway you can get a good steak at some of the O clubs. What about lasagna?"

Lasagna was a brilliant choice. It could easily be made in bulk, in advance, and baked in the mess hall's ovens.

"Will they let us use the ovens?" I asked. "I don't know."

"I guess you'd better find out."

For the next few days the words, *you want to do what???* reverberated in exasperated tones throughout the hospital.

No one had ever asked to cook her own dinner, using the mess hall's kitchen and utensils.

There was no precedent for—or against—it. Eventually the chief cook decided in favor of her venture, but Joanne would have to obtain her own food.

With a little research, she discovered that for a dinner party the size she intended, she could requisition the food she wanted. The supply officer looked askance at the correctly completed form then helped her request five pounds of hamburger, another five of lasagna noodles, and everything else she would need to serve lasagna, garlic bread, and salad to a guest list of 20.

But, he warned, she would have to go get the supplies herself.

At last, there seemed a way to prevent such frivolity. They refused to allow Joanne to requisition a driver to take a jeep to get the cooking supplies from the warehouse on the other side of Long Binh Post.

After giving it some thought she finally told Joanne, "You'll have to take and pass a driver's test, so you can requisition a truck or a jeep from the motor pool."

And, so, Joanne batted her baby browns, and found someone willing to spend an hour teaching a pretty girl how to drive a deuce and a half truck.

She passed the exam, of course.

On the morning of the lasagna party Joanne and Stephanie

requisitioned a jeep, took it across Post to a warehouse that held five pounds of hamburger with her name on it.

Tired at the end of a long string of 12-hour nights, I slept through most of the preparation, but awoke in time to discover the lasagna was in the oven, cooking slowly. I helped Stephanie tear lettuce into big metal bowls, push two picnic tables together, and find two relatively new hospital sheets to use as tablecloths. Using dishes from the mess hall, we set the tables under the covered walkway outside our Hooch.

We gathered a little after 1800. Joanne lit some candles, someone poured the wine, someone else popped a beer. In all we were 16: four nurses, a spy (Nurse Val's husband,) and a Medical Service Corps officer. The rest were all surgeons, including the Chief Surgeon for the entire Army in Vietnam, COL Stuart Roberts, whose living quarters were a short distance behind Hooch 3.

We laughed, we joked, we commended Joanne's ingenuity. We forgot where we were. There were no sounds of outgoing rockets, and no furious whaps made by arriving helicopters filled with wounded. The war was quiet. The lasagna delicious, the company incomparable.

Chapter 15.

WATER BUFFALO BOY

Most of the time our patients were soldiers or Vietnamese civilians caught in the crossfire. But then, toward the middle of the year, Ward 2 received one of the most unusual patients to need their care: a Vietnamese civilian who had been gored by his water buffalo. Had a platoon's intense search for enemy soldiers upset the big animal, causing it to turn on the farmer, who moments earlier had been harnessing its brute force to dig up rice paddies? Had they somehow caused this tragic scene to happen?

There was little they could do. They could not shoot the animal, for if they did it would deprive its owner of his livelihood. The area was "hot" (unsafe) and gunfire would attract unwanted attention. With few other choices remaining they called for a medevac. They did not know the name of the village where they patrolled, only its map coordinates near the Cambodian border.

When the medevac helicopter arrived, flying in fast and low, its crew saw a frightful scene: the father dying, the family wrenched with grief, the soldiers filled with anguish. The men on the ground hurriedly dumped the bleeding farmer onto a stretcher and made the hand-off to the helicopter crew, where its medical corpsmen immediately began attending to their new patient's wounds. This barely took a minute, for there was danger in lurking too long at a hot LZ.

Ready for takeoff, the crew chief mimed a question: didn't they want to send a family member to accompany their seriously injured relative? The family looked around. Elderly parents? A pregnant wife with three other children? An aunt or uncle? As the chopper prepared to spin skyward, someone thrust the eldest child on board. He was ten.

We learned this story from the medevac crew when they came a day later to check on their patient.

I can imagine the conversation that must have taken place between the helicopter pilot and the radio operator in Admitting:

"Hello, 24th Evac, this is Medevac one-three. We are 20 minutes in bound with a civilian on board with chest and abdominal injuries."

"Roger that, Medevac one-three, what are the nature of his injuries."

"Well, he's been gored by a water buffalo."

"A water buffalo? You have to been shitting me... All right, I'll notify the ER to have O neg (the universal donor blood) ready."

At the 24th Evac the general surgeons repaired multiple gores to the man's chest, abdomen, arms, and face—all made by the water buffalo's razor-edged tusks. The man was so severely injured his life lay in the balance for days.

Joanne came by my room to tell me about her newest patient.

"You hear about the guy gored by his water buffalo?" she asked.

"Everybody has. It's unbelievable. Is he going to make it?"

"I don't know Hessel, he is about as sick as anyone I have seen in my time here." She sat down hard on my bed. Joanne was one of the best nurses I knew. If anyone could nurse the farmer through this ordeal it was Joanne."

"Did they tell you about his family member?"

"No, what?"

"It's a child. He can't be more than 10 years old. And it gets worse. They're Montagnards. No one seems to know their dialect. I don't know how to help them."

Vietnam was—and is—a melting pot of astounding diversity: Ethnic Vietnamese who could trace their lineage along the Mekong delta for centuries, ethnic Chinese who had arrived in Vietnam a thousand years earlier but still thought of themselves as Chinese, not Vietnamese. People of French and Vietnamese heritage, whose ancestors had met when Vietnam was a French colony. And a multitude of people belonging to a stir fry of mountain tribes, each with their own dialect, who we generally referred as Montagnards.

The next day I made a point of stopping by Ward 2 to say hi to both Joanne and Stephanie. I was as curious about their new patient as the rest of the hospital.

It was impossible to miss the farmer. Lying in a bed close to the nurses' station he had both arms wrapped in volumes of gauze, suspended by support cradles fashioned from yet more gauze. His chest was one massive dressing. Chest tubes protruded from each side, coiling toward big gallon jugs, partially filled with water, sitting on the floor. This was the closed system necessary to keep his lungs inflated. He had opened incisions on his abdomen and a temporary colostomy. A foley catheter drained his bladder. More penetration wounds covered his legs. His injuries were as severe as anyone who who'd been hit by an exploding mortar shell.

A young boy sat at the foot of the bed. He seemed more resigned than frightened by his surroundings. Unlike other Vietnamese family members, he had no comforts from home. No money, no mat upon which to lie, no food for cooking. Instead he squatted at the bottom of his father's bed, hour after hour, waiting for something to happen.

The Ward 2 nurses immediately recognized the seriousness of the situation. Some of Vietnamese women shared a little food. A night nurse gave him a blanket and pillow so he could be a little more comfortable sleeping on the floor. By the end of the second day the Ward 2 nurses started taking the child a little something to eat at mealtime.

Of all the nurses on Ward 2 Joanne and Stephanie seemed most often to be assigned to care for the father, and by extension the child. If they minded they never let on. Joanne took a real shine to the boy, found him changes of clothes, added his laundry to hers, and brought him down to Hooch 3 to shower ever couple of days.

The boy had to have been on Ward 2 for more than two weeks when LTC Wangerstein learned that the one of the patient's family member was a child. Although she was not unsympathetic to the boy's plight, she was not happy. She didn't have a plan for what to do. She simply no longer wanted him on the Ward. He would have to go.

But where?

Still new to Vietnam I doubt if she had any idea how difficult it would be for the Ward 2 staff to carry out her orders. "Find the boy's village and send him back," she instructed MAJ Lewis.

If only it were that simple. Since no one could communicate with the little boy, who didn't seem to know where he lived, no one could ask him where his home was. The patrol that had called in the medevac was still in the bush; communication with them was spotty. And anyway, all they had were a few map coordinates. There wasn't even a clear record of which air ambulance company had brought the father and son to the hospital.

Finding the boy's home was going to take some time. Nevertheless, LTC Wangerstein persisted. She wanted the boy off Ward 2.

Believing out of sight might have the same effect as out of mind, Joanne brought the boy to our Hooch, where she treated him like a younger brother. During the day, he stayed in her room for several hours, until Colonel Brunhilda had made her rounds and it was deemed safe for the child to come out. Then she snuck him onto Ward 2 so he could spend time with his father.

Joanne made a pallet for him in her own room, where he slept. In retrospect Joanne was fooling no one. Showing she, too, had a soft side, LTC Wangerstein had to know the boy was still there, allowing Joanne to continue with this masquerade.

He was still there when Joanne was to begin a rotation to the night shift. How was she going to care for father and son, yet still get some sleep during the days? The father was slowly regaining strength but still too sick to care for his child.

Joanne asked me if I could look after the boy, but I was about to start a rotation of nights myself, and was not that interested. I didn't want what little free time I had to be saddled by the responsibility of caring for a child. Somehow, with minimal help from her fellow nurses Joanne managed to get through the night shift rotation.

About a month after the father was admitted, with his eventual recovery assured, an American in fatigues with no insignia attached arrived on Ward 2. By his uniform we were certain he was CIA, and the hospital was abuzz with the idea we were being visited by a real honest to goodness *Spook*.

The CIA officer talked briefly to the farmer, who was now strong enough to speak a few sentences, then asked to speak to the child.

The CIA agent and the boy talked for 20 minutes before the agent reported that he thought he could find the child's village.

A week passed, during which the boy stayed with Joanne most nights. His father continued to heal, and was ultimately transferred to Ward 3. The nurses there were quite content to let Joanne continue to mother the boy.

Three days later the CIA agent arrived with a couple of young soldiers and an older Vietnamese man. He had found the platoon leader who had called in the med-evac. The civilian was an elder of the village. He and the boy embraced.

"I'll be back," the agent said.

Someone informed Joanne that the CIA and village elders would arrive the next morning to take the boy home. By then he truly was a younger brother to her, and she cried, knowing she would never see him again.

Chapter 16.
LE ANH PHUONG

Two young soldiers disposing trash heard a mewling sound coming from the interior of the garbage dump. Figuring a kitten had gotten stuck while foraging, one of the young men reached in to release it. Instead of a furry paw he found a human hand attached to a tiny baby girl. She was scrawny, appeared to be of Afro-Asian descent, and no more than two months old. She was naked, and had a big bump and a scrape on the top of her head.

One of the men hastily removed his fatigue shirt and wrapped the baby in it. Back at their Company they quickly swapped the shirt for a blanket and, commandeering a jeep, roared across Long Binh Post with the baby in her rescuer's arms.

"What's her name?" the admissions clerk asked when they carried her inside.

"Hell if we know. Looks like her mother didn't want her anymore and didn't want anyone to know about it." Vietnamese orphanages were filled with children fathered by American men; many of whom were African-American. The Vietnamese were especially prejudiced against children of mixed racial heritage when the father was black. Dumping unwanted children in orphanages was common practice.

Well," the clerk snorted. "I hate admitting her as unknown Vietnamese female infant. She needs a name."

He thought for a moment before combining three Vietnamese names that sounded as though the owner might be a pretty Vietnamese—or American girl. "I know," he pronounced. "Let's call her Le Anh Phuong."

Nga laughed when she heard the name. "That's a man's name," she cried with glee. "You should change it."

But this required more paperwork than the admitting clerk wanted to do. "I named her; it sounds like a girl's name to me," he defended. "Let's keep it."

Someone dug a bassinet out of storage—who knows why we had one in the first place, scrounged some diapers—who knows from where, bathed Le Anh, found some swaddling blankets, bandaged her head, lay her gently in the crib, and transferred her to Ward 5.

Fortunately, Le Anh seemed to have survived her tenure in the garbage dump without serious injury. She had no other bruises except the one on her head, and it wasn't so much a bruise as it was a fluid filled pocket between her brain and her skull where one of her fontanels (soft spot) had yet to close. Bulging fontanels made us pay attention: they indicated increased intracranial pressure, which in turn could lead to brain damage. But fontanels are there for a purpose: to allow room for a child's brain to grow. That extra space was a blessing for a baby like Le Anh.

What we feared most was infection. An anesthesiologist started an IV in one of her tiny veins. And we hung the first bottle of antibiotic rich fluid she would receive during her stay on Ward 5.

Scientists describe a person whose fluid needs are in balance as being in a state of "homeostasis." This is ideal for it means a person's kidneys are functioning properly, and his blood is carrying enough oxygen to his muscles. Deprive a healthy person of water and he compensates by getting thirsty; if he drinks too much he pees. And it is the brain that throws the master switch, directing, in part, things like thirst, rapid breathing, and other mechanisms meant to keep a person alive when his fluid balance is out of whack. Under normal circumstances these compensatory mechanisms kick into gear automatically. But brain damage changes everything. Getting too much fluid is as dangerous as not getting enough.

Small children, infants, and the elderly are not able to compensate for alterations in their fluid balance as easily as adults. Even children with simple stomach viruses often wind up in the hospital and sometimes die from dehydration.

Because Le Anh needed intravenous fluid to get antibiotics, and we did not yet know if she could not tolerate formula, the doctors calculated just how much fluid she needed. Then, as she got better, and started drinking formula, the amount would be decreased. The initial calculation was to give Le Anh 60 ccs of fluid an hour. That's two ounces.

Depending on the manufacturer, IV tubing delivers one cubic centimeter (cc), also called one milliliter, of IV fluid in 12 or 15 drops a minute. This is a perfect flow rate for an adult, easy for a nurse to calculate. But it is a dangerous set-up for a child. IVs are notorious for never running on time. Normal movements cause the roller-clamp to move ever so slightly, or the needle moves inside the vein, bumping into one of the millions of valves inside veins designed to help blood return to the heart.

Instead, pediatrics nurses use IV tubing called pediatric solusets, where the droplet ratio is a 1:1. Sixty drops of fluid, one for each second, deliver one cubic centimeter of intravenous liquid. Much easier—and safer—to calculate.

The pediatric soluset also has built in safety mechanism: Between the main 1000 cc IV bottle and the IV tubing there is a small chamber, holding no more than 150cc (five ounces). When using it properly the nurse fills the intermediate chamber, then clamps off the tubing to the main IV tightly. So even if the IV speeds up, the intermediary chamber prevents a child from getting too much fluid too quickly.

Keeping Le Anh's IV running at precisely 60 cc/ hour turned out to be the most challenging aspect of her care. Despite our hawk-eyed observations of both the drip count and the amount of liquid in the intermediary chamber something went wrong. Who knows whether someone forgot to close the tubing between the chamber and the main IV bottle? Who knows if someone inadvertently opened the chamber? Who knows if someone purposefully sped up the IV? Whatever the cause—could it even have been Mighty Ralph? —just as Le Anh was getting better Carol Ann discovered IV fluid pouring into the baby at a rapid rate.

The excess IV fluid pushed Le Anh over stability's edge. She had two seizures. Jennison put her on Phenobarbital and her condition stabilized.

I may have been the only nurse to have thought that having both clamping mechanisms to Le Anh fail was too much of a coincidence for it to have been accidental. Since Carol Ann had saved the day, and the baby seemed to be doing OK, I kept my suspicions to myself. Perhaps it really was Mighty Ralph; I could not imagine anyone wanting to harm this baby.

By then all the nurses loved the little girl. We made formula from cane syrup and condensed milk and fought to take turns feeding her. When we weren't busy with other patients we rocked her. We wanted to take her home with us. Anything but a Vietnamese orphanage.

Ginny Chang, a Ward 5 nurse of Chinese heritage, whose husband Mark was a Medical Service Corps (MSC) officer also attached to the 24th Evac, was one of the nurses who fell the hardest. She spent all her spare time cuddling Le Anh. Someone jokingly suggested that she and Mark adopt the baby.

To Ginny this was not a joke. She and Mark decided they wanted to have children someday. Why not now? Why not adopt a Chinese American baby who desperately needed someone to care for her?

In 1970 being pregnant led to discharge from the Army. Already having a child in the family was unusual but not out of the question. The young couple lived in a small trailer in a part of the 24th Evac designed for married couples and senior officers. Ginny reasoned she and Mark could hire a Mammasan to babysit Lee Ann Chang when they were at work. She was already a short-timer (someone with only a month or two left in Vietnam.) Ginny could finish her tour of duty in Vietnam before taking their newly adopted daughter home to the States.

They went to the Army Headquarters with their plan. The Army was reluctant, but Ginny and Mark persisted. Within a week they received permission to approach the Vietnamese authorities.

Vietnamese orphanages were already overcrowded with unwanted children. Surely, they would allow an American couple of Oriental heritage to take one small Afro-Asian baby girl off their hands.

Meanwhile, Le Anh continued to improve, and though it was too soon to be certain, it did not appear she had sustained any permanent brain damage. Arrangements to transfer her to a Vietnamese orphanage were initiated. And still no word from the Vietnamese government about Ginny and Mark's request.

On the day before Le Anh was to be transferred to an orphanage in Saigon the government formally denied the Chang's request to adopt the tiny girl. Their reason: no one knew for certain if Le Anh had brain damage. They did not want Mark and Ginny to change their minds and return the baby to Vietnam.

Mark and Ginny protested, but to no avail. The following morning a representative from the orphanage, together with someone from the Vietnamese government, arrived at the 24th Evac. Ginny tearfully handed the baby over to the person in charge. And then she went back to work.

When writing this story I decided to research the name: Le Anh Phuong. This is what I found: It *is* a girl's name:

Le: *tears*

Anh: *intellectual brightness*

Phuong: *one of 4 mythical characteristics of Vietnamese folklore. In this case, the Phoenix.*

I have long wondered what happened to the baby, who would now be in her late 40s. I hope she proved true to her name and rose with intellectual brightness from the ashes on which she was found and the tears her plight caused.

Chapter 17.
PRIVATE ROOMS

During its construction someone had created two small "private rooms" along the far, back wall of Ward 6. They were not rooms so much as enclosed spaces with sides that rose nearly to the curved ceiling of the Quonset hut. Each space held a bed, a small nightstand, and a standard issue over-the-bed hospital table. There was no room for any extra equipment, and no bathroom. Even maneuvering a wheelchair from door to bed, then out, took strategic planning. What the rooms lacked in space was compensated by the simple fact that each "room" had a door that could be opened and closed, thus giving its occupant some degree of privacy. These two rooms were, as far as we knew, the only private rooms in U.S. Army Hospitals outside Saigon, perhaps in all of Vietnam.

A steady stream of high ranking military officers and both military and civilian women came through the doors of Ward 6, shunted there, for its privacy, even if it was limited. Several of our staff, one with appendicitis, another with hepatitis, spent time in our back rooms, too.

LTC Jack Williams came to Ward 6 from USARV (US Army Vietnam) headquarters. Tall, athletic, with just the hint of a paunch Jack Williams was a soldier's soldier. A larger than life lifer, he loved the Army. This was his second tour of Vietnam.

LTC Williams was admitted to Ward 6 with stomach pains a few weeks after the Cambodian incursion concluded. He had been working eighteen-hour days, overseeing the transport, supply, and safety of thousands of men. He seemed to have gotten himself a stomach ulcer in return. A barium swallow showed some areas where his stomach lining looked particularly fragile. We fed him Maalox and bland food, and ordered him to steer clear of too many cigarettes, too much coffee, and too much booze. Sheepishly, he admitted to practically living on the first two substances during "Cambodia." The Chief of Medicine ordered sleeping pills, and the anti-nausea drug Compazine, which has a mild sedative effect.

I was working days on Ward 6 during Col William's stay. Things were quiet, and it was pleasant to be able to talk to a patient who knew exactly where he was. We liked and respected each other, even though he was a lifer, and I made no secret of my belief that we needed to simply pull the troops out and let the Vietnamese squabble over their wretched little country. When he returned to duty I missed our daily sparring.

Three weeks later Colonel Williams was back on Ward 6, throwing up blood. I was working nights then, and volunteered for 6 so I could take care of him.

He did not look well. Still wracked with abdominal pain, he had not been able to keep anything down, even though he had followed doctor's orders.

On the second night, I went to check on Colonel Williams around midnight. "How's your pain?" I asked.

"Worse. And it seems to be really bad right around here," he said, placing his hand over his left breast. I checked his pulse. A little rapid, perhaps a little irregular. I checked his blood pressure. It was OK. I was a surgical nurse, yet I knew the symptoms of a heart attack and LTC Williams's symptoms seemed to be quacking.

"Do you have any heart problems?" I asked casually, not wanting to frighten him. But the Colonel was not stupid.

"No. I don't think I am having a heart attack. There is no elephant on my chest."

Still, I was nervous. When the opportunity arose I wandered over to Ward 7, the medical unit, and shared my concern with their night nurse. "I think he could be having a heart attack," I said in a tone that I hoped indicated I really needed her help.

There was always a bit of tension between the medical and surgical nurses. We got the glory, and reveled in it. But their patients were just as sick as ours, and there were no easy cures for malaria, venomous snake bites, or black water fever.

My compatriot on Ward 7 followed me to 6, where she accompanied me to LTC William's room. She listened to his heart, took vital signs, quizzed him about his pain. The one thing she did not do was an electrocardiogram. The machine was too damn big to fit through the door. She offered LTC Williams a comfortable chair near her nurses' station so she could do an EKG. He refused, believing we were making entirely too much fuss over him.

She returned to Ward 7 with instructions to call her if anything changed. I dragged a chair into the room, and for much of the night, I watched LTC Williams's chest rise and fall rhythmically while he slept.

The Chief of Medicine was furious with all of us the next day, for the EKG tracing showed that the Colonel indeed had had a mild heart attack. The next evening he was gone from his bed in Ward 6, and lay, instead, next to the nurses' station on 7, the twelve "leads" of an EKG machine glued to his back and chest. When I visited him, he thanked me, but also insisted I'd over-reacted, that he'd been in no real danger.

A week later, his doctor decided the Colonel's heart attack had earned him an early trip home. The afternoon before he left, he found me, doing vital signs on Ward 6.

"You saved my life," he said.

"I don't think so."

"You trusted your instincts and kept me alive overnight."

"If I had really trusted my instincts you'd have been on the medical ward at 0300," I replied.

He encircled me in a giant bear hug. "Listen, Barbara, we both know the truth. I'd like to repay you if I could."

"Can you get me out of this place?" We both laughed.

"No, but you know, I do have some pull with the people at ANC (Army Nurse Corps) Headquarters in D.C. If you don't like your next duty assignment let me know and I'll get it changed."

Three months later I received orders for Ft Gordon, GA. I did not know this was the home of the most beautiful spring in the east, only that the hospital at Ft Gordon was an old cantonment facility, not especially popular with younger nurses. By then I had had a letter from LTC Williams reiterating his offer to get me a choice assignment. Carol Ann had been notified she was going to Ft Knox, KY. We decided to go together. COL Williams fixed it. If it hadn't been for his heart attack I might never have met my husband Jim, who I met at Ft Knox.

Miss Edith Andrews was newly retired from a fifty- year career in nursing. A small, round ball of pure energy, she had never married, and lived alone in an apartment outside Chicago. To celebrate her retirement she had decided to travel around the world; her method of transportation: a merchant ship that sailed into many ports around the globe, including Saigon Harbor.

The ship had just completed its docking maneuver and was still offloading cargo when Miss Andrews took one misstep and broke her left ankle. She wound up in one of the private rooms on Ward 6.

Miss Andrews was not thrilled with her newfound status as patient on Ward 6. Neither were we. We couldn't understand how she had wound up at an Evacuation Hospital rather than the Army Hospital in Saigon. She was loud and demanding, far more work than the truly sick men who had been wounded in war. And, she had absolutely no concept of how fortunate she was to be sent to a U.S. Army Hospital and not to one of the poorly equipped, poorly staffed, and poorly cleaned Vietnamese hospitals.

We had no call system except for a small bell which sat on her bedside table. Miss Andrews rang it constantly: fluff my pillows, rub my back, get me something to drink. *Pay some attention to me.*

We often fought over who would be stuck as her nurse. And I, always an easy mark, often lost.

"But Hessel," someone once argued, "she likes you."

"No she doesn't," I retorted. "Just yesterday she told me I was the worst nurse she had ever met!"

Getting Miss Andrews in and out of bed, whether it was to use the toilet or take a shower, was like trying to thread bulky yarn through a cross stitch needle. She barely fit in a wheelchair. She was so short and so stocky she couldn't even help push herself out of bed to get into the damn wheelchair. Then relishing in the attention—

didn't she know I had other patients?—she washed every inch of skin with meticulous care. My job was to rub her back and feet with lotion.

She fussed incessantly about her bed linen being itchy, the temperature of the ward, the infrequent changes of water in her pitcher, and the food not being good enough. Wishing to be finished assisting her—until she needed to use the bathroom yet again—I squirmed in frustration as I waited while she completed each morning's ablutions. How I longed to tell her off, then go take care of someone who really needed me.

Older now, and wiser, I appreciate Miss Andrew's sorry plight much more than I did then. She didn't have a TV to watch, a book to read, or crossword puzzles to do. Her dream vacation had ended badly. She was bored, sore, and angry.

Someone from the cargo line arrived at the 24th Evac with her suitcases and a check for several thousand dollars. He was sorry to inform Miss Andrews that the ship would sail the following morning without her. She would have to find her own way home. Her dream vacation had ended with a bang and a whimper. Always good for strange chores, Peg Lewis helped Miss Andrews buy a ticket to Hawaii as soon as she could fly.

In contrast, Donna Ernst, whose situation was much more serious than Miss Andrews, asked very little of us. Also a nurse, Donna was a Baptist missionary, living and working near the Cambodian border. Married, and the mother of three children, including a 10-month-old baby, Donna came to the 24th Evac after she discovered a lump in her breast.

The general surgeons biopsied the lump and discovered Donna had breast cancer. They suggested she go home, where she could receive the best treatment for her cancer, giving her the hope of recovery. But Donna refused. She devoutly wanted to stay with her family—her husband and children, and the people of the village their mission served. She would take her chances without chemo if the doctors would do a radical mastectomy. Whatever the outcome she was not afraid to meet her Lord.

The doctors argued against doing this invasive procedure in

Vietnam, where the risk of infection was extremely high. "You are young, your children need you."

"My children are in the Lord's hands, as am I."

"Go to Manila. We'll see to it that you get into an Army Hospital. It's a modern facility. Not meatball surgery, like this." (We quickly adopted the term 'meatball' after seeing M*A*S*H.)

"I trust you," Donna argued. Finally she said, "If you won't do the surgery I'll just go back to the mission."

This we could not allow. The doctors operated, cutting a deep incision, excising as much tissue as they could in hope that they would remove every cancerous cell from her body.

Donna stayed at the 24th Evac little more than a week. Once we removed the sutures she decided she no longer needed to take up a bed.

We lost touch with Donna, but a few years later, someone who knew I had been at the 24th Evac asked me if I had cared for *that missionary woman*.

When I answered that I had indeed cared for Donna Ernst, she told me the surgery had been unsuccessful. A year later the church recalled Donna and her family to the States. It was too late. A few months after her return, she indeed went home to meet her Lord.

Chapter 18.
FEMALE PROBLEMS

One of our doctors was MAJ Ramon Hernandez, who had been drafted part way through the residency that was to make him an obstetrician-gynecologist. The Army made him a general surgeon, so most of his patients were men. A kind, quiet man, Dr Hernandez convinced the Army to open a clinic for the women of Long Binh Post. There he spent one afternoon a week, seeing nurses from both of Long Binh's hospitals, the enlisted women's barracks just down the road from the 24th Evac, female civilian employees and Red Cross volunteers. It was not especially challenging for someone who wanted to deliver babies for a living, but we nurses were grateful. Mostly MAJ Hernandez dispensed birth control pills, and treated countless yeast infections, probably caused by spending too much time in the hyper-chlorinated water of the nearby swimming pool.

Most of us thought the high point of his experience in Vietnam was presiding over the birth of a Vietnamese baby, the child of one of our mammasans, who came to work in early labor. Someone had tried to send the mother home early in the day, but she didn't want to go. By the time her work was done she was in hard labor and could not go. Unwilling to tie up necessary staff to assist Dr. Hernandez in the delivery, MAJ Lewis went from ward to ward, asking for volunteers.

Things were quiet enough on Ward 5 that day for Ted to give me his blessing to go to the OR to assist with the delivery. There were a couple of other nurses, too. At the time, I had no desire to be a maternal-child nurse. I just wanted to see a birth. Once we prepared the OR, the mother was ready to push, and within a half hour gave birth to a healthy baby girl.

Then she and her new daughter went home. Because she had been born on a US Army Post, the baby could technically be considered a US citizen. But we issued no birth certificate, and I do not think the mother cared. She had given birth in healthier surroundings than she would have at home.

No one, not even MAJ Hernandez, expected he would have a second, more interesting birth to attend before his year in Vietnam was over. Then surprise—and controversy—took over when one of the ER nurses went into labor.

Although she was petite, her fatigues completely hid Ellen's pregnancy. No one knew she was pregnant until she announced, while assisting an ER doc in a minor procedure, that her water had broken. Like everyone else at the 24th Evac, MAJ Hernandez was stunned by the news that one of our nurses was about to have a baby. Even he hadn't noticed the bulge in her belly. But his major concern was that Ellen had had no prenatal care.

"Don't worry," she told him, as the two prepared for her to labor in one of the unused operating rooms, "I've been taking prenatal vitamins. I've listened to the baby's heartbeat.

Everything will be fine." She estimated that she was in the 35th or 36th week of pregnancy. The baby would be premature, but, with luck all would be well.

The labor progressed without problems and in the late afternoon Ellen gave birth to a baby girl, Elizabeth, who weighed a little over five pounds. As soon as mother and baby were recovered from the birthing experience Ellen and Elizabeth were transferred to one of the private rooms on Ward 6. I was their nurse.

Caring for them was easy. We found Le Ahn Phuong's bassinet and more diapers. We didn't need formula because Ellen was breastfeeding. The baby latched on right away, as if she knew she had no choice but to get the hang of breastfeeding from the very beginning.

"Who's the father?" Peg Lewis asked.

Then Ellen explained the extraordinary circumstances surrounding her marriage and pregnancy: Ellen was not, as most of us thought, engaged to a B 52 bomber pilot stationed on Okinawa. She and her husband had married in secret before departing to a war zone.

Ellen's first duty assignment after Officer's Basic—we were in the same platoon together—was Brooke Army Medical Center at Ft Sam. San Antonio was also home to two Air Force Bases and between the three huge military complexes there were plenty of opportunities for young, single, well educated, junior officers to meet. Ellen met Bill, immediately fell in love, and the rest should have been an easy history. A B-52 Bomber pilot, Bill already had orders for the US Air Force Base at Okinawa. If they married, Ellen's request to accompany her husband would most certainly be granted because she could easily work at the U.S. Army Hospital there. They could live together as husband and wife.

But things were not that simple. Both young lovers had recently lost their fathers, and their newly widowed mothers, perhaps fearing that either Ellen or Bill could be killed in Southeast Asia, wanted the two to wait until they returned to the States before marrying. But Bill and Ellen did not wait; instead they married in secret.

"Bill has no idea I'm pregnant and neither do our mothers," Ellen told Peg Lewis when the supervisor went to check on her nurse who was about to become our patient.

The news Ellen was pregnant and in labor spread through the hospital like wildfire. The typical response: *What was she thinking?* Why hadn't she told Bill? He managed to get to Long Binh at least once a month to see Ellen. How had he not noticed his wife's changing figure?

And there was controversy. The women generally agreed it was foolish for Ellen not to have told Bill—or to have had no prenatal care, but thought it romantic that Ellen chose to stay in a war zone when she could have taken the easy way out, going to Okinawa.

Almost to a man, the guys complained that if she had been *his* wife they would be unable to completely trust her again.

There was, of course, a third explanation: that Bill knew about the pregnancy. But fessing up at this late date posed certain risks to a career in the Air Force. Only Bill and Ellen knew for certain which version of the story was true, and they weren't telling.

It really didn't matter. What did was making sure Ellen and the baby received proper care, Bill got to his wife's beside as soon as possible, and the paperwork establishing Elizabeth's birth was properly recorded.

Peg Lewis flew into action. She burnt up the telephone wires between Vietnam and Okinawa, finding Bill, helping Ellen inform her husband of this newest alteration to their lives.

Bill managed to get to Vietnam when the baby was less than 24 hours old, easy enough for someone with access to an endless variety of flights to Saigon or Bien Hoa. Then came the hard part: calling their mothers. Their marriage license was stored at Bill's mother's home. To issue a valid birth certificate the Army wanted a notarized copy of it.

Hi Mom, how are you? Guess what? We got married after all! Guess what else? You're a grandmother! The new mothers-in-law and grandmothers took the news with surprisingly good humor.

Then another problem arose. During the delivery MAJ Hernandez had routinely drawn off some of the baby's blood from the umbilical cord. Testing it for blood type, the lab soon discovered baby Elizabeth was type O with a positive Rh (Rhesus) factor. Ellen was O, Rh negative. Ellen needed a shot of Rhogam.

This blood product blocks the mother's immune response to the Rhesus positive factor in the baby's blood, should their blood have inadvertently mixed during pregnancy. A life-saving medication, Rhogam prevented babies from developing what was once called "blue baby" syndrome (its medical term is erythroblastosis foetalis). It would do nothing for Elizabeth, but giving a shot of Rhogam to Ellen would protect her future children.

Peg was in her glory trying to find some Rhogam, which needed to be administered within the first 72 hours after delivery. There was none to be had at any US Army facility in Southeast Asia. Then Peg located some at the US Air Force Hospital in Manila.

"You have 72 hours to get it to Vietnam, and the clock is already ticking," she instructed.

The person on the other end of the line objected, citing the expense of Rhogam and the difficulty in transporting it within the required time period.

"Listen," Peg practically shouted into the phone on Ward 6, "this baby is half Air Force, now get it here."

It arrived well within the critical time frame to protect Ellen and her future babies.

Ellen and Bill completed the paperwork identifying them as husband and wife, changing her name, and issuing the baby her own unique birth certificate. Although controversy echoed through the walkways and Quonset huts of the 24th Evac, we were much too busy to seriously care about whatever kind of trouble either Ellen or Bill might find themselves in once the dust settled.

However, the junior officers did bear the brunt of some minor repercussions. Colonel Brunhilda was embarrassed she had not noticed the pregnancy. Ribbed by her fellow senior officers, she saw it as a reflection of her leadership capabilities; Brunhilda even threatened to have each nurse parade in front of her dressed only in our skivvies. We retaliated by finding even wilder socks.

Chapter 19.
THE PURPLE PAPPASAN

During the Vietnam conflict members of the Army's Medical community reached out to civilians living near our posts to provide much needed medical care. For the average doctor or nurse this meant going on "MEDCAPs" (Medical Civilian Action Programs) —organized visits to Vietnamese villages where medical personnel volunteered their time to diagnose disease, teach basic hygiene and disease prevention. We also provided villagers with soap, creams to treat skin rashes, and antibiotics to fight infections.

Some of the staff went on several MEDCAPs; others refused, believing most supplies would immediately be handed over to the Viet Cong.

I only went on one MEDCAP, on my day off, fairly early during the year. Our destination was the village of Long Binh. Accompanied by a few men from an infantry unit, whose role was to protect us from enemy attack, we doctors, nurses, and corpsmen assembled our equipment then piled into the back of a Deuce and a Half truck.

We rumbled down the paved roads of Long Binh Post, out the front gate and into the Vietnamese countryside, bumping along dirt roads until we found ourselves in the real Long Binh. It was a tiny village of houses built on stilts above rice paddies and marshland. There were one or two unpaved streets, and, as far as I could tell, no store, no community center, or way of communicating with people outside Long Binh. The village was quiet; many of its residents were already at work on Long Binh Post. But a few of the hamlet's elders and a gaggle of curious children proudly showed the curious

Americans around their tiny town.

Eager to receive our attention, the villagers then lined up waiting for their turn to see the doctors who were kept busy looking at skin rashes, sore throats, and even some potentially broken bones. We nurses were in much less demand.

It was exciting to off post, to see what a Vietnamese village was like, but eventually I got bored. We didn't get back to Post until mid-afternoon. It seemed like a waste of my one day off that week.

After I returned home I wondered about my disinterest in getting to know the Vietnamese people. I had spent my senior year of high school as an exchange student, living with a family outside the suburbs of Copenhagen. I had fallen completely in love with Denmark and her people, and had eagerly learned Danish, one of the world's most difficult languages.

How was it possible, then, that I had so little interest in knowing the Vietnamese? The people with whom I came in contact were friendly, polite, cheerful. I liked them, and they seemed to like me. Yet, I willingly encapsulated myself on Post, or limited trips off Long Binh to other American facilities. Yes, I did go to Saigon a couple of times, hitching rides on helicopters bound for the South Vietnamese Capitol. I even visited The Third Field Hospital. But, like the trip to Long Binh Village my visits to Saigon turned into hot, boring days with the added anxiety of knowing I would need to find a safe ride home.

Eventually I decided my response had little to do with the people and everything to do with the War. I did not want to fall in love with the Vietnamese in the way I had fallen for the Danes. I could not bear to watch the dying of a people I might truly come to know, perhaps love. I already was caring for all the combatants in Vietnam, including Americans, Koreans, Thais, Australians, and Vietnamese on both sides of the war. I had watched little Bi's mother cradle her dying daughter in her arms. It was enough for me to bear.

After Cambodia, when things on Ward 5 were particularly quiet, one outreach clinic patient made his way, albeit reluctantly, to the neurosurgical unit. He was scheduled to have brain surgery two days later. To me he will always be *The Purple Pappasan*.

Getting report that evening, I listened in amazement as the day nurse described our newest patient, tucked into a bed on Ward 6. He was Vietnamese, a seemingly kind and loving grandfather and great grandfather, perhaps even a great-great grandfather, for he was 94 years old.

He had gone to one of the outreach clinics earlier in the day because he was having trouble seeing and wanted glasses. But when the doctors examined him they discovered a brain tumor pressing on his optic nerve. They decided to do surgery.

I was appalled. Why not give this elderly gentleman a pair of reading glasses—something he probably had never owned—and tell him he would see much better? Instead surgery was scheduled for two days later.

Midway through my shift that night I decided my eyes were too tired and irritated to continue wearing my contact lenses. I went to my cubby hole located in the passageway between 5 and 6, looking for my glasses. They weren't there. I thought I had left them there a few days earlier, and now I was worried. They were the only pair of glasses I owned. I ran down to my hooch, checked the top of my dresser and bedside stand, but they weren't there either. I looked in the boxes surrounding my cubby in case I had put them in someone else's mailbox by mistake. Still no glasses.

I whined to Carol Ann, "What am I going to do? I can't see without my glasses." "Why don't you look in the Pappasan's bedside table?" one of the corpsman suggested.

"He came here looking for glasses."

Surely, they would not be there. Surely, he would know that these glasses, designed to correct my extreme nearsightedness, were not for him. But I looked anyway. And there were my glasses, sitting inside the top drawer. I removed my contacts and placed my glasses firmly on my face. I would not let them out of my sight until the Pappasan had surgery.

Two evenings later I arrived at work to discover the old gentleman lying in the bed closest to the nurses' station, his head bandaged in layers of gauze. The surgery had gone as planned but the Pappasan was in a light coma. It would take much longer for him to recover than the doctors, used to working on 20-year olds, had anticipated.

Nevertheless, everyone expected the old gentleman to recover slowly.

By the end of the week the Pappasan was conscious, though sometimes difficult to arouse. Like all the other neurosurgical patients he was to have nothing by mouth, standard procedure on Ward 5. It was the rare patient who was sufficiently alert to be fed safely. A depressed level of consciousness could easily lead to choking on food, and then to aspiration pneumonia, an ominous complication.

After surgery patients need to move and eat. It helps them expand their lungs, maintain muscle, and repair damaged tissue. We knew this, but we were so used to taking care of 19-year- old men with plenty of reserves to weather days without food or walking we forgot the Purple Pappasan was not our average patient.

Instead, we followed our usual routine: infusing antibiotic loaded intravenous fluid into the old man's veins at the usual rate of 100 ccs/hour. After about two weeks the elderly gentleman began to protest, telling our Vietnamese nursing assistant he was hungry. Worse, he was thirsty. Nga, whose patience with her fellow countrymen was unpredictable, simply laughed off the Pappasan's complaints.

I was medication nurse on the day shift when things came to a head. Twenty minutes after I'd hung a new IV, I passed the old gentleman, now sitting cross legged on his bed, a
satisfied smile covering his face. Then I noticed a few drops of blood on his previously clean sheets. I looked up to the IV bottle I had just hung. It was completely empty. There was no water on the bed or the floor.

"Damn it," I reported to Ted. "I think the old geezer just drank his IV." "No, that's not possible."

"The IV is dry, the tubing is completely shut off, and he is smiling." I burst out laughing. "Tell Jennison we've got to feed him now." I got a new bottle of fluid, changed the IV tubing, and wrote down 1000 cc in the spot for accounting oral intake on the proper flow sheet.

Two days later my suspicions were confirmed. For the Pappasan now suffered from a terrible case of diarrhea. Drinking a liter of sugar water containing 20,000,000 units of penicillin, which in turn would kill the normal bacteria in his intestinal tract, was the most logical explanation. How else, after two weeks of having nothing to eat or drink could we explain the diarrhea? Then he developed thrush, a yeast infection of the mouth that often plagues people taking large doses of antibiotics.

We had few medications on hand to treat severe diarrhea and most were ear-marked for men with dysentery. That left Tincture of Paregoric. But the doctors were hesitant to prescribe it because it contained morphine and could make the old gentleman confused. The few drugs the pharmacy carried to treat yeast infections were not meant for oral use. Thus, we were forced to rely on the same therapy my mother had used on me as an infant, Gentian Violet. An effective method for killing the yeast spores that cause thrush, Gentian Violet also stains everything it touches a brilliant purple. Sitting cross legged on the bedpan, waiting for another bout of diarrhea, his lips stained the color of blueberries, he resembled a skinny, purple Buddha.

I felt sorry for the old gentleman. I didn't know if he could see better, but I seriously doubted brain surgery was what he had had in mind when we went to the clinic a month earlier. In an open ward with absolutely no privacy, he sat for hours on a hard metal bedpan, covering himself as best he could by throwing a sheet over his head. Although he muttered to himself he never complained.

After the thrush was better, his mouth not so sore, we began feeding the Purple Pappasan small quantities of rice and vegetables. He began walking around Ward 6 as vigorously as he had before the surgery. Finally, we sent him home. With a pair of glasses.

Chapter 20.

MORE MEMORABLE PATIENTS

Disseminating Intravascular Coagulopathy—DIC—is a terrible complication of infection, surgery, bleeding and certain complications of childbirth. In DIC the blood's normal clotting mechanisms fail, resulting is unremitting hemorrhage. Without appropriate treatment, victims of DIC bleed to death, even as they are being given pint after pint of blood.

I first learned about DIC at a conference decades after I left the Army. As I listened to the lecturer describe the litany of failed clotting functions that happen in DIC, I immediately thought of a patient who had died in my care on Ward 5. Could DIC be the reason we could not save this man's life?

He was a Colonel in the North Vietnamese Army, admitted to Ward 5 with serious injuries including a depressed skull fracture. As the night shift staff listened to report we were astounded to learn we had an NVA officer as a patient. None of us could ever remember having a North Vietnamese soldier on our unit. The POW hospital, technically a free-standing entity staffed by nurses and corpsmen from the 24th Evac was in the process of closing. At the same time is was obvious that this man needed skilled neurosurgical care if he was to survive. To refuse to care for him like any other patient would be a dereliction of a duty we were asked to perform, and a complete disregard for the oaths we had taken as graduate nurses and doctors.

He may have been fighting with the North Vietnamese, but we knew nothing about the person. We had no way of knowing if he agreed with his government, had been conscripted into the North Vietnamese Army, or came from a long line of military officers. We didn't know if he had a wife and children, a house, a car, or even a pet. I am not certain we knew his name. Only that he was the enemy.

Now, there was another enemy lurking: Death. To be sure there were probably people in the hospital that night who wanted him dead. But that was not our concern. *Our job*, like it or not, was to try to save this man's life. And it would be a challenge. In addition to the skull fracture he had multiple frag wounds to his chest, abdomen, and legs.

And he would not stop bleeding.

We had seen this before: Men whose condition should have been stable, but were bleeding heavily. We pumped blood into them as fast as we could, even if a complete blood-type match had not been made. It seemed to me that the more blood a man received the more likely it was he would die. Yes, needing a lot of transfusions meant the man was seriously injured, and might not survive no matter what. But I thought something else was involved.

Once, when we were not busy, I did my own completely unscientific study, in which I looked at the medical records of men who had died of hemorrhage rather than their wounds per se. Just how much blood had each received? Although my study population was small, it appeared as though the magic number was sixteen. Men who got more than sixteen units of blood shortly after being wounded just didn't seem to make it, even if we had tended his wounds. I thought it might be the sodium citrate added to donated blood to extend its "shelf life."

Our NVA patient might have been a North Vietnamese soldier but we tried to keep him alive as valiantly as we did any American patient. As he continued to bleed someone suggested we try giving him a pint of fresh blood. And for that we needed a donor.

More than usual, the hospital seemed to be teeming with people that night: the staff, men coming in from the field looking for a decent meal and some company, others waiting for their compatriots to be released from the hospital following emergency treatment, helicopter crews getting a brief respite between missions. Word we needed fresh blood spread quickly throughout the hospital. Several men offered to donate—until they heard that the recipient would be an NVA soldier.

After unsuccessfully recruiting a blood donor we tried another approach: our supply of blood was rapidly being depleted. We could not afford to use any more on an NVA soldier, yet we were morally obligated to try to save his life.

It worked. Someone in from the field offered to be a donor. We placed him on a stretcher, found the necessary equipment to draw five hundred milliliters of precious fresh blood into its container. As soon as we were finished we gave the blood to our POW.

It didn't work. An hour later, after receiving a total of seventeen units of blood the Colonel died.

Although caring for an enemy soldier on Ward 5 was a rarity, we took care of all combatants—and their victims—on Wards 5 and 6. Because they were our allies, Korea, Thailand, and Australia all sent men to Vietnam. The Australian presence was sufficiently large they had their own hospital. We loved caring for the Aussies. Most had concussive injuries, and thus were on Ward 6, waiting for their foggy brains to clear. Once I was flirting with an Australian Lieutenant until his commanding officer arrived, whisking him to the Australian hospital.

Another patient was a feisty Korean who, startled from a nap, jumped on top of his bed, his hands poised as if he carried a machine gun, and started screaming at an enemy only he could see. After a dose of IV valium he dosed off, and when he awoke remembered nothing about his previous behavior.

The Thai soldiers were good fighters who always made us laugh. Standard operating procedure in the Emergency Room was to cut the fatigues from the body of any wounded person, so he could be turned from side to side and front to back in search of wounds that might otherwise might be missed.

Once, soon after I arrived in Vietnam we had a mass casualty involving ten Thai soldiers who were bent over a hand grenade when it exploded. Because their injuries were to their head and face they were ferried to the 24th Evac.

One of the ER doctors on duty that night was new, as was one of the nurses. The rest of the ER staff delighted in assigning them to the first wave of Thais to come through the door. The Newbies were both shocked and amused to discover that, to a man, the Thai soldiers wore women's silk underwear. I don't think this had anything to do with their sexual preference, but rather reflected how they felt about silk next to their skin. Silk, like wool, breathes, and thus is a good fabric choice for undergarments in tropical countries like Vietnam or Thailand. No doubt the men had many shopping choices when they were home, but in Vietnam the only silk underwear available, that would also fit, was made for women. It was always good for a bit of gallows humor to cut fatigues from a Thai soldier to see him lying on the stretcher, wearing a pair of hot pink undies.

After the Cambodian Incursion things were so quiet we discussed reducing our workload from seventy-two to sixty hours a week. Or perhaps we would continue to work six days a week, but our shifts would only be eight hours long. For the first time in months we had time to take care of all patients the way we would have liked: more frequent position changes for bedridden patients, conversations with men on Ward 6.

Into this quiet came Major Conrad, admitted to Ward 5 after a piece of shrapnel pierced his forehead, severing his optic nerve. He also had two broken arms. These were wrapped in gauze—not casts—and suspended from the metal tubing for IVs. Unlike most of our patients on Ward 5 the major was awake and alert, completely aware of what had happened to him. It must have been terrible for him. Because he couldn't see us he had to trust we were caring for him properly. Because his arms were immobilized he couldn't scratch an itch, or feed himself, or do any of the other things people with good arms strength take for granted. And yet he was one of the most considerate men I met during that year.

One very quiet afternoon I asked the major if there was anything I could do for him. His reply: "could you write a letter home to my wife for me. But please don't tell her I am blind."

I was happy to write to Mrs. Conrad for her husband, writing what he dictated to me. I explained I was writing instead of the major because he had two broken arms. I didn't lie. I just didn't tell the complete truth. She wrote back before her husband's recovery took him to the States, thanking me for taking good care of her husband. I had no regrets about not telling her MAJ Conrad was blind. They would need time together once he got home to face the reality of his situation, their situation, and hopefully, then, adapt.

Most of the men on Ward 6 were there because of closed head injuries. Many recovered and returned to duty within a week or two. Today, neurologists and neurosurgeons recognize that having a concussion is not necessarily a simple injury. The dizziness, headache, blurred vision, and confusion caused by a concussion can last for weeks. But in Vietnam, when men showed no overt sign of injury we had no choice but to return them to duty. Sometimes, when symptoms lasted for more than two weeks, we were able to send patients home.

One such patient was a handsome young *grunt* (the Vietnam version of G.I.) from Long Island, who had sustained a very bad concussion. He was a sweet kid who worried whether he would be sent back to his unit or home. The first time I cared for him, shortly after his arrival on Ward 6, he remarked that I didn't smell like any soldier he'd ever met before. Wearing perfume, in my case Estee Lauter's "Youth Dew," was sometimes a double edge sword. It helped patients identify me as a woman first and a soldier second. But others could become nauseated if I dabbed on too much perfume before leaving for work.

When our young New Yorker was still dizzy and seeing double after two weeks Dr Jennison decided to send him home. A month later I received a letter from him. He was on an in- patient unit at a Veteran's Administration hospital, still recovering. He remembered me because of my perfume. And he wanted to thank me for taking such good care of him.

Soon after the Purple Pappasan went home we cared for a young ARVN soldier who had a head injury. He also had gas gangrene in one of his legs.

Gas gangrene is an infection caused by a germ in the Clostridial family of bacteria. It is present in the soil, and sometimes in the human intestinal tract, and if it enters the body through a deep cut it produces toxins, which in term kill surrounding tissue. Unless

Outside isolation for patients with gas gangrene

treated, often by amputating the affected limb, as was done in World War I, where gas gangrene was rampant, it can cause a fatal septic shock.

Clostridial bacteria cannot live in the presence of oxygen. In 1970, a new treatment for gas gangrene was emerging: place the patient in a super-rich oxygen environment like a hyperbaric chamber and pump in oxygen. If the Navy hospital parked off the coast had a hyperbaric chamber we certainly didn't know about it. But we knew how to improvise. If we could get extra oxygen into his wound, now sliced open to allow for secondary healing, perhaps we could save his leg.

After a meeting in which the entire staff agreed that our patient had nothing to lose— and neither did we—Zak and Howie moved our gangrenous soldier, together with his bed, dressings, IV, and an enormous oxygen tank into the quadrangle outside our door during the day, hoping the fresh air would have a slightly better percentage of oxygen than our Quonset. There, they created a make-shift lean-to from screens and extra blankets, dressed the patient in pajamas with the left pant leg cut away, and taped the oxygen tubing to the

MAJ Peg Lewis at outside isolation area

young man's thigh, poising it so the oxygen would flow freely over the gangrenous area. This created the most oxygen rich environment we could think of.

While monitoring him carefully for signs of worsening infection, we kept the oxygen flowing until it was clear, after about three days, that our treatment wasn't working, and the young ARVN soldier's condition was deteriorating. We transferred him to Ward 9 after the orthopedic surgeons worked hard to create an above-the-knee stump for his now amputated leg. At least he might have a fighting chance to get a prosthesis, and lead a normal life.

Chapter 21.

GALLOWS HUMOR

Funny things happen in a war zone even if war truly is hell. Sometimes dealing with war's endless horror requires humor. To illustrate this point, MAJ Mary Quinn described how she and her nurses of the 71st Evacuation Hospital used humor to make it through the dark days of the 1968 Tet Offensive:

"Humor played an important and vital role in maintaining morale during these trying times and it was encouraged on every level. Without it we may have lost control of situations. Getting together in little groups and recounting the funny things that happened relieved tension on several specific occasions."*

Fortunately, 1970 did not bring a Tet like the one two years earlier. For us it was simply the Vietnamese New Year's celebration, and one that slipped by without much notice. Mostly, like the nurses at the 71st Evac we found humor in every day experiences, from reading cartoons like *Hagar the Horrible* to smiling about the Purple Pappasan.

Consider caring for *Unknown Vietnamese Female #1* on the first morning in April.

As the day shift arrived for work that morning the people on nights looked especially grim.

"It's been a hectic night," the nurse giving report began. "We have a new Vietnamese patient, a woman. She's on a vent (ventilator) so we don't even know her name. We've been calling her "Unknown Vietnamese Female Number One" until somebody can find out what her real name is." The nurse's voice was raspy with exhaustion.

"Why, what's been going on?" someone wondered out loud.

"Let me give report on the rest of the patients. Then, I think the best way for you to see just how sick she is, is for you to come with me to her bedside. She has a lot of stuff wrong withher and the docs have written several consultations. It's going to take most of the day for you to get them filled."

After letting out groans, we pulled out paper and pen, ready to take morning report on all our patients, including *Unknown Vietnamese Female #1*.

Finally, the charge nurse began to describe this new patient. "The last patient is *Unknown Vietnamese Female #1*. She was brought in during the night after a rocket went off near her village. She has a depressed skull fracture, two collapsed lungs, a gash in her abdomen that extends to her pelvis, and two fractured legs. She's on a vent, has two IVs running, one with whole blood at 150 ccs/hour. The neurosurgeons did emergency surgery last night, but they couldn't address all her problems."

The charge nurse handed Ted a consult form before continuing. "She needs casts on both legs. That's the consult for orthopedics I just handed you." She picked up a second, and then a third form. "They think her abdominal injury might extend to her uterus so she has a consult for Dr Hernandez, and here's one for the general surgeons." She handed more forms to Ted, "Her nose is broken and a piece of shrapnel might have punctured her frontal sinus, so here's one for Kelly," she said, referring to Dr. Dave Kelly, the ENT specialist. Then she handed Ted the final form. "Oh yeah, we think she might also have malaria, so here's one for internal medicine."

"Good grief," someone muttered, "how is she still alive."

"There are some irregularities in how they inserted the chest tubes. I think you should follow me so I can show you." We stood, and trooped behind the nurse.

Unknown Vietnamese Female #1 was swathed in gauze from her head to toe. She hardly seemed real. And then we realized she wasn't. The breasts beneath her pajama top consisted of two small metal bowls. Her arms and legs were vinyl covered lengths of wood, meant to hold IVs in place on patients' arms. Oh, she had two IVs and chest tubes alright, but the red liquid in the chest tube and one of the IVs was made of food coloring. It was April Fool's Day and we had just been skunked. Royally.

As we laughed about the absurd joke played on us by the night crew we decided to continue with the gag. Most of the surgeons thought she was funny. Dr. Isaac Gielchensky, a thoracic surgeon and Holocaust survivor, thought it was so funny he filled out the consultation form. Only the Chief of Medicine reacted negatively, chiding us for wasting his time.

By noon everyone at the hospital had seen our "patient." The joke had been the perfect antidote to a busy day.

According to *A History of the Army Nurse Corps* the Chief Nurse of Vietnam, COL Patricia Murphy, who had laughed heartily at my desperate need to pee that first afternoon in Vietnam, had a terrific sense of humor.* Once she sent her chief nurses sets of darts and dartboards with a picture of herself at the bullseye.

As she was nearing the end of her tour of duty in Vietnam COL Murphy visited every Army facility where "her" nurses served. A date for her farewell party at the 24th Evac was determined. Next, how to bid COL Murphy goodbye. Somehow, Susan got stuck with the chore of planning an appropriate send-off from the junior nurses.

Instead of a somber affair, Susan decided we needed to "roast" the Colonel. So, we prepared a skit. Together with Joanne and Stephanie—and myself—we wrote a ten-minute skit filled with nonsense: an exhausted nurse ready to go home (Joanne,) a bouncy new nurse ready to take her place (Stephanie,) a hospital's harried chief nurse (me,) and COL Murphy (Susan.)

Not sure what the Colonel's response would be we four practiced nervously. We employed the old phrase, "what can they do, send us to Vietnam?" when we wondered if we were going too far in our roast. We did not tell COL Brunhilda, or the two Pegs of our plans.

On the evening of COL Murphy's farewell all the 24th Evac nurses not on duty reported to the Officer's Club. Serious speeches praising the Colonel's leadership filled the Club's smoke-filled air.

Then it was our turn. As we four—Susan even looked like COL Murphy with her gray streaked wig—began our routine. COL Murphy howled with laughter. She thanked us for avoiding one more serious goodbye and made sure we five had our picture taken together. She also sent Susan a gift: the gold oak leaves worn by a

COL Patricia Murphy's farewell party.
L to R: Susan as COL Murphy, Barbara as Chief Nurse, COL Murphy, Joanne as an over-worked staff nurse, Stephanie as the new kid

Major in the Army. Accompanying the insignia was a note thanking us for an entertaining evening, offering the oak leaves to Susan should she stay in the Army. COL Murphy chose correctly. Of the four of us Susan was the only one to make the Army Nurse Corps her career. When she made Major she wore the oak leaves proudly.

The hospital received its water from a treatment plant somewhere on Long Binh Post. Afterward it went into a large water storage tank that stood beyond the mess hall. It held more than enough water to supply the hospital with clean water for eating, drinking, bathing, and toileting needs for about 36 hours. Most of the hospital's bathrooms were connected to an enormous septic system. That storage tank and leach field were beneath the patchy grass between the two sides of the hospital.

Making sure our water and sanitation needs were met was the job

---

* Both quotes are from *A History of the Army Nurse Corps* written by COL Mary Sarnecky.

of the Haliburton Corporation of the Vietnam War: Pacific Gas and Electric (P, G, &E), a branch of the same company that had supplied my apartment with electricity back in San Francisco.

P, G, & E had a large compliment of American engineers working to maintain the physical plant of Long Binh Post. But the day to day operation of the 24th Evac fell to a handful of under-trained Vietnamese employees.

These were pleasant, hardworking people, who came through the gates of Long Binh Post every day, or night, submitting to the indignities of being frisked for drugs and contraband, and they did their jobs as best they could. But their living conditions at home were definitely third world. Moving from home to work must have been a little like taking a daily travel through time.

The complexity of our equipment was sometimes beyond the P, G &E's employees' know-how to operate flawlessly. More than once we lost water during the night because a P, G & E employee had unknowingly thrown the wrong switch, shutting off the water—or worse yet, causing it to flow directly into the septic system. Sometimes their inexperience caused us to lose electrical power. With six ORs in near constant use this was a terrible problem——until someone managed to scrounge a back-up generator. But it was the plumbing that gave them—and us—the most problems.

When our Vietnamese housekeepers and maids, walked through Long Binh's gates each morning, they brought rice and vegetables with them to cook for lunch. Whatever they did not eat was tossed down the drain, usually of one of the shower stalls. The mammasans then cleaned the shower stall, but rarely used enough water to flush their leftovers into the septic system.

When food got stuck the entire drainage system got clogged. More than once I got up to pee in the middle of a day's sleep to discover a P, G, & E employee, plumbers' snake in hand, trying to unclog the drains of Hooch 3.

Most of the time we took the periodic interruptions of our sewage system with good humor. It was not the Vietnamese employees' fault we had come into their lives, attempting to drag a people whose outhouses hung over nearby streams, into the 20th Century. The entire concept of a septic tank large enough to hold the bodily waste of about 500 people may well have been beyond their ability to imagine.

Most problems took only an hour or two to fix, and were annoying, not dangerous. But once we came within hours of having to temporarily close the 24th Evac, transferring the patients and most of the staff to other hospitals, because one too many Mammasans dumped her leftovers down the drain.

This time it started in Hooch 2, which was fortunate for those of us in 3 and 4 because we could still use our bathrooms. The snake method of unplugging the drains seemed to work at first, but then the mass of rice, vegetables, poop, and Vietnamese fish sauce rolled itself toward the center of the compound, plugging each bathroom in succession.

The first afternoon it seemed as though the P, G & E workers would be able to find the problem and correct it easily. But after digging up miles of drains they were still unable to find the blockage. COL Cochrane formally ordered the staff to conserve water, bathing only those patients in need. We nurses were told to use the flush toilets in our hooches only when absolutely necessary. (Thank goodness for my coffee can.) Two shower stalls in the enlisted men's quarters were given over to the nurses to use late in the evening and then early in the morning. Even the showers in Hooches 3 and 4 were off limits.

On the second day, the problems were still not fixed, and COL Cochrane closed the hospital to incoming wounded. Even seriously injured neurosurgical patients would have to be treated elsewhere. It simply wasn't healthy to add new bodies to this ever-worsening sanitation problem.

Then, COL Cochrane contacted his superiors at USARV (Army headquarters for all of Vietnam) as well as the commanding officers of nearby hospitals. If we still had no plumbing at 1400 the following day we would begin transferring patients to other facilities. The logistics of packing up about 300 patients and another 200-300 health care providers would be enormous, but COL Cochrane felt he had no choice.

Doctors, nurses and corpsmen were told to pack a couple of

changes of uniforms and other necessities we could grab at a moment's notice once transferring patients began. On Ward 2, where Joanne and Stephanie worked, each nurse was assigned to attend specific patients during the transfer.

Meanwhile, the P, G, and E employees worked even harder, searching for the blockage. Part of me hoped they would not be able to solve the problem in time. Excited about seeing something other than the 24th Evac I eagerly packed my duffel bag, even though I only wanted to be gone a day or two.

I was off the following day, but had already wandered on down to Ward 5 a couple of times to check my mail and see how things were going. I had even meandered by Ward 2 to see how Joanne and Stephanie were preparing for the transfers. Too busy to talk, Joanne agreed to meet for lunch in the mess hall at 1230.

We were part way through lunch when a loud boom reverberated through the hospital compound. It sounded as though we had taken a direct hit from an incoming rocket.

Not quite.

However, the bathroom between Wards 5 and 6 *had* taken a direct hit. In their desperate rush to unblock the sewer line before 1400 the P, G, & E men finally found the problem. They decided the fastest way to get rid of the blockage was to blow it into the septic tank. They rigged an air pressure hose designed to send a couple of hundred pounds of pressure screaming through the septic system. And flipped the switch. The explosion we heard was the sound of the mass shooting through one of the toilets on Ward 5. The force of it was so strong it blew apart the porcelain bowl, spewing rice, vegetables, and shit on every bathroom surface, including the ceiling.

Howling with laughter we quickly spread the news that the transfer to other hospitals was cancelled. Ward 5 would not be opened for new business until the bathroom could be thoroughly cleaned, but the rest of us were back in the war.

Chapter 22.
A DIFFERENT SORT OF BLOW-UP

Desperate to fill the needs of an overworked Army Nurse Corps, Congress enacted legislation in mid May 1969 directing the Army to admit new graduates with bachelor degrees in nursing as First Lieutenants. The legislation came a few days after The Walter Reed Army Institute of Nursing graduated its second class, and so at our commissioning ceremony, in the rose garden of the Surgeon General of the Army, we swore to protect and defend the Constitution of the United States as Second Lieutenants.

It took a while for the directive to filter down from Army Nurse Corps Headquarters in Washington, D.C. Even then some chief nurses refused to acknowledge that their young, inexperienced college educated nurses were in line for a promotion. It wasn't having a bunch of First Lieutenants that bothered them so much as it was knowing that, given the temper of the times, promotion to Captain would come a year later—before we had been full-fledged nurses for one full year.

May came and, in a small ceremony conducted by LTC LeBlanc Joanne, our classmate Lynn, and I were dutifully "pinned" with the silver bars of a First Lieutenant. We took our uniform blouses to the tailor who changed the embroidery from black and gold thread to black and silver. Not a single thing about our lives changed other than our pay.

About two months later, the 12th Evac sent us a female nurse

Pinning of my CPT bars

with an appendicitis to recover from surgery in one of Ward 6's private rooms. Walking back to Ward 5 after lunch I ran into another WRAIN '69 grad, who had hitched a ride to Long Binh to visit her sick friend. We hugged as we greeted each other with surprise: "what are you doing here?" followed by a quick, "I didn't know you were in country." Then I noticed my classmate's collar, which sported the double bars of a captain.

"How did you get those?" I asked, pointing.

"Didn't you know?" she asked, then explained the changes in regulations. Furious, I stormed onto the Ward, searching for Ted. "A friend of mine is here visiting from the 12th Evac. We graduated together. And she's a fucking Captain." I had difficulty keeping my anger from reverberating through the ward, causing a scene.

"Oh," Ted's reply seemed calm, but concerned. "Did you know anything about this?" I demanded. "No."

"I'm going to the Chief Nurse's office right now. Don't try to stop me."

MAJ Lewis ushered me into her office, seating me before her desk. "What's bothering you, Lieutenant?"

"Why am I not a Captain?" I asked.

"What do you mean?" She sat back in her chair, arms across her chest. "I'm supposed to be a Captain and so are Joanne and Lynn."

"What makes you think that?"

"Because I just saw one of my classmates and *she's* a Captain." I kept my voice as calm as I could but I wanted to scream.

Peg got up from her chair and invited the Chief Nurse into the room. Together they explained that all chief nurses in Vietnam were uncomfortable with this new regulation and had decided to wait until we had more experience before making us captains.

"Well the chief nurse of the 12th Evac obviously didn't get the memo," I pointed out.

"You are dismissed, Lieutenant."

I found Joanne and Lynn, and poured out my frustration over this extraordinary slight. And it was a slight. We were graduates of the Army's show-case school of nursing. Joanne had been the honors graduate of WRAIN '69, and not simply because she was smart. All three of us gave outstanding patient care to the most gravely ill patients. Rank Hath more Than Its Privileges (RHIP); it has prestige, power, and pay.

We three returned to the Chief Nurse's Office where we pled our case. To no avail.

But we did not give up our fight for what we believed was right. Eventually, we struck a deal. In exchange for making certain our personnel files accurately reflected the correct date of rank, and we got back pay in a timely manner, we would agree to be First Lieutenants for six months. Then we would be promoted to Captain. We may have sported single black bars on our uniforms but deep down we knew we were Captains. It took a while for the paperwork to catch up with us, but we each received about $1000 in back pay just before Joanne and I were to go to Hong Kong on a week's leave. It was money well-earned and even better spent.

As Thanksgiving approached LTC Wangerstein called for another ceremony. This time we happily received our Captain's bars—and more back pay.

When I arrived at Fort Knox, my duty assignment after Vietnam, I discovered my fight with my superiors at the 24th Evac had been worth every word. Assigned to work on the male surgical units at Ireland Army Hospital, I discovered I was the second ranking officer on the ward—by three days.

Once again I found myself defending my rank as a Captain, when our head nurse, a Major, received orders for Hawaii. Everyone assumed her assistant would become a head nurse. The assistant—I no longer remember her name—had not been to Vietnam, and thus did not have the intensity of experience in surgical nurse that being in Vietnam supplied.

My co-worker was so sure she would become head nurse she began to make plans for how she would manage about 70 patients, spread out over three wings of the hospital. I was not particularly fond of my compatriot, although I am sure she would have been a fine head nurse. So I pulled rank, and thus, became the youngest head nurse Ireland Army Hospital had ever seen.

Fortunately, my experience in Vietnam, and plus using Ted's wise counsel, provided me with the know-how I needed to become a good head nurse.

Chapter 23.
COPING MECHANISMS

Twentieth Century Fox released its hit movie *M*A*S*H*, an irreverent look at War, viewed through the lens of America's involvement in Korea, in March 1970. Richard Hooker's book, upon which the movie was based, had become a best seller long before the movie arrived in Vietnam three months later. By the time we got to see the film, sitting together in the crowded Officer's Club, I had lent out my copy of the book several times.

After seeing *M*A*S*H* I wrote home about it, encouraging my parents to go see the movie. Although *M*A*S*H* depicted a far different situation than Vietnam there was just enough gore, just enough hanky-panky, and more than enough gallows humor that I thought seeing the movie might help my family understand something about my life in Vietnam.

Afterward, my mother wrote that she was going to write the Pentagon and ask for my immediate return to the States if the 24th Evac was anything like the 4077th MASH. For days afterward my friends and I spent our evenings laughingly creating lurid, but accurate, descriptions about what our lives were *really* like to send home to Mom. We never mailed them. The Army would not send us home, and some things you just couldn't tell Mom.

Very few non-medical people understood what it was like to work in a hospital in the midst of war. Technically we were REMFs (Rear Echelon Mother Fuckers,) but ours was not the country club existence of officers sitting in air-conditioned buildings looking for ways to keep busy.

When I Die I'm Going to HEAVEN

Ours was a war within a war, in which we fought—not to kill the enemy—but to keep everyone alive. Platoons came and went on patrol, seesawing back and forth between the intensity of being in the bush and the relative peace of being back at base camp. They suffered unimaginable physical hardship brought on by bad food, bad feet, exposure to the elements, and the constant stomach churning anxiety of thinking the enemy might be near.

We had none of that. We were far removed from the fighting. We had cool rooms, warm beds and good food. We also had a constant, unrelenting stream of wounded coming through our doors, victims all.

And when we needed to renew our own souls we had each other.

After I returned home, I had some dental work done at Ft Knox. The dentist knew I had just returned from Vietnam and every time I sat in his chair he quizzed me about the 24th Evac. "I hear you had some pretty wild bashes over there."

I did not know how to reply. The answer was not a simple yes or no. A description of our antics a la Hot Lips Houlihan and Hawkeye would not help either. Our relationships with each other were much more complex than that, and in a way I was not certain I could—or wanted—to clarify.

The enlisted men smoked grass. I shared a toke or two with a couple of Spec 4 (one rank above Private First Class) research scientists, both PhD candidates whose draft deferments had run out, and who were now studying tropical diseases at the Walter Reed Army Institute of Research satellite facility, located in a building next to the morgue. But I didn't like the loopy feel marijuana gave me. I enjoyed visiting the guys, but I really did not inhale.

Hard liquor was cheap and plentiful, whether purchased at a Post Exchange or in an Officer's Club. A Johnny Walker Scotch cost about fifty cents in our O Club, which was frequented by serious drinkers from the hospital staff, or men in Long Binh for a brief respite, searching for a little conversation with a round eyed woman, and bored, tired, or overwhelmed nurses looking for a little respite too.

My friends in the Medical and Medical Service Corps liked weirdly concocted punches made with rum, vodka, and fruit juice, and enjoyed throwing *Purple Alerts*. The name for these parties was a play on the alert system designed to warn of us of a possible attack by the enemy. Green meant peace, orange "be alert," and red an attack was eminent. In a *Purple Alert* the goal was to get at least a little tipsy on the heavily liquored hot pink liquid as quickly as possible.

Purple Alerts were like frat parties on steroids, attended by grown men and women, who, day in and day out held the lives of countless innocents in their hands, and wanted to forget, no matter how briefly, the damage bullets and bombs could inflict.

I went to *Purple Alerts* because I enjoyed my friends' companionship, but I usually took a book with me, and rarely had more than one drink. I was not being a prude. I had had my share of weirdly concocted punches in college, and simply thought it easier to work a twelve-hour shift without the hangover going wild at a *Purple Alert* might risk.

I also tried to avoid becoming intimately involved with the men around me. Chances were the doctors and Medical Service Corps officers were married, the enlisted men were off limits, and the helicopter pilots primarily interested in casual sex. I was still a newbie when it came to intimate relationships and getting sexually involved with someone I would either see every day in a work situation or might never see again was something I wished to avoid.

So, when my dentist quizzed me about the parties at the 24th Evac I just laughed. I refused to talk about them. My standard line: "you wouldn't understand."

And he wouldn't. For most of the time, having sex—when it happened—was a sort of emotional release that far exceeded the need for healthy young adults to exercise their hormones. When relationships happened, it was because of need. How could I explain to my curious dentist that until he had poured every ounce of skill he possessed into saving the life of a *boy* only for him to die as soon as the surgery was over, or the blood stopped running, or the number of casualties made it necessary to move on to another patient, that being intimate with another human being was not casual, but the giving and receiving of solace? How could I explain that, with rare exception, the intimacies shared were borne of the simple need for another person's touch, and not caused by a wandering eye or a flaw in a marriage?

How could I explain that the parties were wild because during the day we had to be in absolute control? That we used alcohol the same way he would use Novocain: to dull an ache that otherwise would not

When I Die I'm Going to HEAVEN

go away. Or that the sex, drugs, and rock 'n roll of Vietnam in the 70s had little akin to the sex, drugs, and rock 'n roll of the counter culture back home in the States? We were not practicing free love because we could. Rather, we were looking for love in the only place we had.

Many of my friends made peace with the probability that they would find the comfort they needed in the arms of a married man. Carol Ann even had a name for it: Vietnam Marriages.

Not every nurse fell into the arms of a doctor—married or not—just because we worked terrible hours and saw horrible things. Some of us already had serious relationships with men who were either stationed elsewhere in Vietnam, or waiting for us back home. And most of my fellow nurses who fell into Vietnam Marriages were not foolish enough to think the relationship they'd developed out of need would lead to permanence. Nevertheless, once or twice a month we watched tearful good-byes, then held broken hearted friends whenever *he* went home. It was rarely the reverse.

Perhaps some of my fellow nurses were Lesbians and fell into each other's arms at night. If that were the case I never knew. My closest friends and I told each other we loved each other on a regular basis. But ours was not "Eros," or sexual love, but a comforting mix of what the ancient Greeks called *Philia* (friendship) and *Agape* (unconditional) love. Once someone started a rumor that Joanne and Stephanie were lovers, probably because they had heard the two, who worked in the surgical ICU, say the words *I love you* after a particularly hellacious shift.

It stung at first because in 1970 homosexuality was considered to be a form of mental illness. But they laughed it off, while Susan and I and some of our other friends told them and each other *I love you* in such loud and certain terms that the rumor died a sudden death.

For the first few months I was in Vietnam I steered clear of relationships with men. I had a crush on a corpsman from Ward 3 who'd been drafted out of graduate school. He was tall, blonde, and funny. In civilian life we were equals, but in Vietnam a relationship with him could spell serious trouble. When I finally overcame my inhibitions, filching a couple of condoms from the storage room on Ward 5, he rebuffed my advances. Not because he didn't care about me, but because he was almost ready to rotate back to the States. He could see there was little to gain by having an affair during his last few weeks in Vietnam.

Decades later I would come to understand that part of my hesitation in becoming intimate with him—or any other man in Vietnam—was because I had built thick, high fortress walls around my feelings, unwilling to let very few men in. My reason was simple enough: I had left more than my heart in San Francisco. I had also left my virginity. I lost it in the worst possible manner: to a surgical resident who had a reputation as a playboy, conquering nurses whenever he could. His methods were as old as humankind: get her drunk and wear her down. Afterward I felt terrible regret that I had succumbed to his wiles.

Many years later I learned our night together qualified as date rape. But in Vietnam, still recovering from the trauma of what might have been a real rape during basic training, I had neither the time nor the psychic energy to analyze what had happened to me at Letterman. I only knew I wanted a relationship on my terms. I didn't especially want permanence, or the promise of a future together, but I did want respect.

And then I met Tom.

He was not a doctor, but a nurse. He was taller than me, with reddish brown hair that curled around his neck, an inch or so longer than regulations allowed. Like me, he loved reading and classical music, and was amazed I knew the difference between off sides and encroachment. I was a died-in-the-wool Steelers fan. He loved the Cowboys.

Once we discovered our mutual interests the rest was inevitable. Tom invited me to the club for a drink. We talked about everything and nothing. When he walked me the 10 feet to my hooch, I invited him in. He kissed my forehead, my closed eyes, my neck. It was a done deal.

A week later Tom invited me to spend the afternoon in "the love nest," a tiny air-conditioned room under the eaves in one of the male officers' quarters. At the end of the afternoon he proposed.

I accepted.

He gave me a man's well-worn garnet ring he claimed had been in his family for years.

At dinner that evening I found Dr. Hernandez. Could he give me a prescription for birth control pills?

"Are you sure?" Ramon asked.

"Oh yes," I said happily, "we're going to get married!"

I was filled with joy, dancing on air, delighting in the smallest pleasure. I was loved. I was not a conquest. I was more than a warm breast upon which to cry. I was adored, worshiped, desired.

Midway through a long day shift, Major Lewis called me into her office. Without preamble she announced, "You need to break it off with CPT Murray."

"What, why?" I wailed. "You know we're engaged."

"You can't be," she said, her face grim. "He's already married." She handed me his personnel file. There, in the box for next of kin was the name *Angela Murray*. Relationship: *wife*.

As I stood up to leave, I did not know whether to thank the assistant chief nurse or curse her. Instead, I stormed to Tom's hooch, where he was sleeping between night shifts.

I pounded on his door, screaming, "wake up, wake up."

"Barbara." Tom seemed genuinely surprised to see me. "What is it?"

"You're married." I shouted.

He pulled me into his room, which I had never seen before. "Who told you?"

"Lewis, who else?"

Tom sighed. "Yes, technically I am still married. But we're separated. It seemed like the gentlemanly thing to do, you know. Keeping my ex on my medical benefits while I'm over here. Don't worry about it, babe. I still love you. I still want to marry you."

But he never touched me again. A month after he returned home he sent me a letter from the generic post office address at Brooke Army Medical Center, rather than his home's. The letter was impersonal. Its address, not from his home, infinitely telling.

I did not write back. I threw the ring in the trash. And added another row of blocks to the fortress.

Chapter 24.
SICK TO DEATH OF SICKNESS AND DEATH

Dressed in shorts, tee shirts, and flip flops, Carol Ann and I sat on lawn chairs, feeling the warm breeze of an early tropical evening wash over us after yet another long day on Ward 5. The air was redolent with the smell of Vietnamese food cooking and shit burning. The night was alive with sound: crickets chirping, loud music blasting from a stereo inside the Officers' Club, and the thud of outgoing rockets pounding a distant target.

Carol Ann propped her feet on the arm of my chair, her pink-painted toenails brushing the glass that held my rum and Coke. I pulled out cigarettes, offering one. We lit up and sucked deep on the mentholated nicotine.

"What are you going to do, Barb?" I did not need to ask, *about what?* I already knew to what Carol Ann was referring. Having arrived in Vietnam within days of each other, we had toughed out the full six months on the neurosurgery wards needed before we could ask for an internal transfer. If we wanted to go to another part of the hospital our requests would now be granted.

"I wish I knew," I said, sighing. "You know how I feel about working with Ted. I can't imagine having another head nurse. But the patients…" I let the sentence trail off. Carol Ann didn't need me to elaborate. She knew how difficult it was to deal with the ward's daily dose of death and destruction as well as I.

"What about you?"

"I made my mind up today. I'm going to ask for a transfer. I love Ted too, but he's short," she said, referring to the fact that Ted had only a month left in country.

"I guess if we're going to do it, now would be a good time," I said. We were concerned with more than who would replace Ted when he went home. We also needed to consider what transferring out of Ward 5 would mean to our relationships with our fellow nurses.

The Ward could not lose two nurses to internal transfer. We would need to be replaced. Transferring to Ward 3, for example, meant a nurse from the surgical unit would wind up in the neuro ICU. It might make getting through the rest of the year a little easier, but it would win us friends.

But, as fate would have it, the winding down of our involvement in the war gave us a brief window in which to make our decision without pissing off our colleagues: the 12th Evac was in the process of closing. A couple of their nurses had always been transferred to the 24th Evac. Ward assignments were in flux. If Carol and I did not ask for a transfer within the week, a nurse new to the 24th Evac might garner a prized assignment while we stayed in our version of Hell.

"Where you gonna ask to go?" "Oh, the ER, I think."

I pushed Carol's foot off my arm rest. "You can't ask for the ER, that's where I want to go. And I've been here longer than you."

She laughed, then put her foot back on my chair.

Two nights later I arrived on Ward 5 to discover Ted was also working. "What are you doing here?"

"Oh, I thought I'd see how much of a slacker you are on nights," he joked. The reality was two nurses were on leave. We needed Ted to plug a hole in the night nurse schedule.

"Maybe it'll be quiet and we both can take a nap." It was anything but.

Both wards were packed with patients; the men on Ward 5 seriously GORKed. The space across from the nurses' station reserved for the sickest patient, our little ICU within the ICU, was filled with four new patients, each so severely brain injured he needed a ventilator to breathe. Two were American, two were Vietnamese. The two Vietnamese were not expected to live, but the two Americans might pull through.

Zak and Howie were both on duty, taking turns cursing out Mighty Ralph. For if the census was any indicator Mighty Ralph was screwing us royally.

A little after 0100 the machine ventilating one of the Vietnamese hiccoughed, then alarmed. Standing nearby, Zak quickly stepped to the bedside, checked the ventilator, looked at the patient, and announced in a stage whisper, "This one's gone."

He and Howie began post mortem care: removing tubes, washing the body, closing the eyes, then placed it in a heavy green vinyl body bag before carrying it to the morgue.

They had been back less than twenty minutes when a second ventilator alarmed. The second Vietnamese soldier was dead too. Neither man had known what hit him, nor had there been time to notify their families.

I was sad, yet relieved. No one expected them to live. Their dying made my night a little easier. Or so I thought.

At 0300, Zak strode to the nurse's station, where I sat finishing the paperwork needed to transfer our two dead ARVN soldiers to the proper Vietnamese authorities.

"L.T., we have another goner," he said matter-of-factly. I followed him to the bedside of a young American whose admission exam indicated severe brain damage. We had held out little hope for him, even if he had been breathing on his own. Now his respirations were raspy and irregular. Death rattled in his throat. Another corpsman joined us. Someone held his hand. In a moment he was gone.

At 0400 a third ventilator, this one belonging to one of the new Americans, alarmed. I got up to check it. The fourth man was dead.

I walked back to my chair in the nurses' station and picked up my pen. But I could not write. The words describing this man's death simply would not come. I pulled my cigarettes from my shirt pocket, lit up, and took a deep drag.

Ted eased his chair, which was facing the slumbering patients of Ward 6, closer to mine. "Are you OK?"

"No...," I stammered quietly. "I hate this. All this death." I started to cry.

"I think you should leave."

"But I don't want to desert you. I know this job. I like it here. I just hate all the death."

"You are 23." He paused a moment then continued, "Don't worry about me. I'm a tough old lifer. I'll be fine. You need to take care of yourself."

"OK." I picked up my pen and began to write in the newly deceased soldier's chart. Ted had made the decision for me. Relief washed over me.

Before breakfast that morning, I went to find LTC Wangerstein. "I have been a nurse on Wards 5 and 6 now for more than six months. I want a transfer to the ER."

"We have an opening on 15." The Colonel smiled brightly, believing she was offering me a gift by sending me to a unit where many of the patients were sweet Vietnamese children recovering from cleft lip repair. Sometimes they stayed on the ward for weeks. Their childish antics filled the entire hospital, but especially Ward 15 with joy.

"No, not there. If you can't give me the ER or Pre-op, just keep me where I am."

"I don't understand. If you hate Ward 5 so much why go where the wounds are fresher?"

"I think I'd be bored on 15," I said. How could I explain that I had become so accustomed to the acuity of the neuro ICU I feared life without it? How could I explain to the Chief Nurse that as much as I hated the unending parade of brain injured patients I feared dullness more?

I had become a trauma-junkie. I needed my speed.

A few days later Carol and I got our transfers: she to the E.R., me to Ward One. I would make the move after I returned from a week's leave in Hong Kong.

Chapter 25.
THANK-YOU MR. FINK

The limo driver held the back door of the big black Rolls Royce open for Joanne, Carolyn—our friend from the 93rd Evac, and me. Open mouthed, we looked at the wide front doors, rimmed on each side by a large sculptured Chinese lion. This was the grand entrance of Hong Kong's Peninsula Hotel. This was where we would be staying for the following seven nights.

We had asked the hospital chaplain, who had been in Hong Kong three weeks earlier, if he could make reservations for three at the Hilton. But the Hong Kong Hilton was busy that September, filled with American soldiers on leave, and guests from around the world visiting both Hong Kong and Tokyo for the Japanese Exposition.

"I got you reservations at a place called the Peninsula. I didn't see it, but the desk manager at the Hilton assured me you would like it a lot." Without any of us knowing it, the chaplain had made reservations for us in Hong Kong's premier, and thus five-star British Hotel.

As he opened the front door, the concierge smiled. "Welcome to the Peninsula, we are happy to be your home away from the war," he said with a faint British accent as he nodded at the green everyday dress uniforms we wore.

After seven months in fatigues and combat boots our skirts, stockings, and high heel shoes felt peculiar. Pulling our overseas caps from our heads, we walked across the hospital lobby, crowded with guests drinking afternoon tea. Even with eyes fixed on the front desk we could not help but notice the many stares turned in our direction. American women in military uniform were not commonly seen in the elegant lobby of the Peninsula Hotel.

The front desk clerk looked at us and smiled. "Welcome, ladies. You must be Lieutenants Hesselman, Kane, and Schilling. We are delighted to have you." We showed our orders, which we used in lieu of passports, and signed the guest register.

"Let me take you to your room. Because you are very special guests, we have made one of our largest rooms available to you. I think you'll like it." He smiled, wrinkling his nose, pleased to be part this happy performance.

When we reached 'Room 412,' the clerk turned the key, opened the door, and held it so we could have our first look at the luxury that would be ours for the following week. The room was enormous, at least the size of four hooch rooms melded together. Two double beds and a large cot with a deep mattress were arranged beautifully, the double beds on the corridor wall, the cot under the front window. Three comfortable arm chairs, a writing desk, and lamps in various shapes and sizes helped fill the room, which did not appear to be crowded at all. A large vase of fresh flowers sat on the writing desk.

"I'm sorry we had to put a cot in here, but we didn't have any extra doubles," he said. "It's fine, more than fine," we murmured stunned by the elegance of our surroundings. "Let me show you the bathroom." The desk clerk entered the room, and opened the last of three doors on the wall to our right. The bathroom was easily as large as one of our hooch rooms, its walls covered by tiles the color of warm sand. The toilet and vanity were lovely, high quality bathroom fixtures, but it was the bathtub that took our breath away. Easily bigger than a king-sized bed, the tub was partially sunk into the tiled floor.

"I think I'm in heaven." Carolyn threw herself onto the cot, spreading her arms as if she were making an angel in the snow.

"If that will be all ladies, I'll leave you to unpack."

"Wait a minute," Carolyn jumped up, fumbling in her purse for some of the Hong Kong dollars we had gotten at the airport.

The desk clerk smiled, "Thank-you, but no, it is my privilege." He waved her away and closed the door behind him.

On our own, we feasted on the sights and smells of the room one more time before someone declared, "Before we have dinner I want a bath."

"Let's find a drugstore. Maybe we can get some bubble bath."

Twenty minutes later we appeared again in the front lobby, this time dressed in civilian skirts, blouses, and sandals.

"Is there any place opened where we could find bubble bath?" we inquired of our friendly front desk clerk. He gave us directions to an apothecary he thought would still be opened this late Sunday afternoon.

More heads turned as we strolled through the lobby with its tables, which we learned later were part of the hotel's restaurants. People who had seen us arrive grinned at our metamorphosis.

The following morning we made our way to the lobby, where we sat down and ordered breakfasts of eggs, fresh fruit, scones, clotted cream, and strawberry preserves. Dressed for the day in Bermuda shorts and lightweight cotton blouses we discussed our plan of attack for our first full day in Hong Kong. It could be summed up in one word: Shopping.

"Girls, girls, over here." We turned to see a short, balding American eating alone. "Please, come over this way, if you don't mind." He waved.

Joanne led the way.

"You girls aren't by any chance in 'Room 412,'" he asked.

"Yes, how did you know?"

"I was in 'Room 412' until yesterday morning. Then the management asked me if I could move to a smaller room so they could accommodate three US Army nurses coming in from Vietnam. I'm guessing that's you." His accent was both nasal and broad, straight from New Jersey.

"We're sorry you had to move," we replied as one.

"I'm not. It's something I could do for our brave women soldiers in uniform." I thought it was a line, but in fact our smiling benefactor was sincere.

His name was Irving Fink,* and he was indeed from New Jersey. A middle-aged salesman, he traveled the world buying and selling leather and leather products. He had been in Hong Kong on business for nearly a week and would return the States the day after we were to return to Vietnam.

"Where are you girls headed now?"

"Shopping!"

We all laughed.

During that year in Vietnam we were entitled to a week's leave and a week of R&R—Rest and Relaxation. Soldiers in serious relationships combined the two into a trip to Hawaii, where they spent precious moments with wives, husbands, and sweethearts. Those of us who were single tended to take leave and R&R as two separate vacations with Hong Kong and Australia as choice destinations.

For men, being in Hong Kong was about buying electronics and partying with willing Hong Kong women. For us it was about shopping, shopping and sightseeing, shopping and eating good food. Did I mention shopping?

As a port where east met west Hong Kong itself was a shopper's mecca. But savvy soldiers knew where to find the very best prices: at the big US Navy Base Exchange on one of Hong Kong's many islands.

The Navy BX was a shopper's dream, and we each had lots of dreams to fulfill. Except for payments on cars currently being used by parents and siblings back in the world, none of us had debt or anything of significance on which to spend money. We each had amassed what seemed like a small fortune to spend on our shopping spree, one we had been planning for months. Then there was the $1000 in back pay Joanne and I had just received.

We had done our homework, talking to others at the 24th and 93rd Evacs who had already gotten their big reel to reel tape players, speakers, TVs, and cameras. We knew what we wanted: for me it was a TEAC reel to reel tape deck and matching speakers, a TV, and a 35 mm SLR camera with a telephoto lens.

—

*Irving Fink was his real name. I will forever be grateful for his kindness.

By noon, we had made our electronic purchases and arranged for them to be delivered to the Peninsula, which was on the mainland. Then we hit the jewelry counter. All of us wanted Seiko watches, which we snapped onto our wrists as soon as our selections were made. But there were more goodies to be had: strands of Mikimoto pearls, matching earrings, star Safire necklaces, and rings. Opals, diamonds, emeralds, and pagoda rings in every height and color of semiprecious stones imaginable.

Not knowing what I was buying, I purchased three twenty-two-inch stands of five-millimeter Mikimoto pearls, one for my mother, one for my sister Laura, and one for myself; two star Safire rings for my younger sisters Martha and Susie, earrings and a right-hand ring to match my pearls for myself, an opal and diamond ring and matching, dangly earrings.

A host of Chinese shops, filled with trinkets, souvenirs, and silk in every color of the rainbow lined the hall leading into the main PX. You could have a hand tailored dress or suit made during the week. As someone who had been sewing her own clothes since she was 12, I wanted some of that silk. Standing before the glossy fabric, I could not make up my mind which color or weave to choose.

Exhausted from our long day, and laden with heavy packages we trooped back into the Peninsula. Mr. Fink looked up from his table, which he now shared with a beautiful, raven haired Chinese woman, who we would learn later, owned a factory that specialized in carry-on bags.

"How was it?" he called.

"Wonderful," we bubbled over with excitement, describing our purchases. "You must be tired, how 'bout I buy you dinner!" he declared.

"Oh no, we couldn't possibly..." one of us began.

Mr. Fink interrupted, "I have another business dinner across town. Eat dinner here. I will tell them to put it on my tab."

And so that night we dined on vichyssoise and steak au poivre and drank champagne in the Peninsula's fanciest restaurant.

On Tuesday we went sightseeing, visiting pagodas and Buddhist temples. We wanted to go to Hong Kong's famous floating restaurant, rumored to have the best Chinese food in the entire world. But we were nervous about it, having heard one too many nurse describe the diarrhea from which she then suffered, a tourist's revenge.

A ship of the British Royal Navy sailed into Hong Kong's Harbor. Carolyn met one of its officers who invited her to tour the ship and some of the sights of the British Crown Colony.

Joanne and I decided on a different plan: we intended to take a train through the New Territories as close to "Red China" as we could get.

In 1970 China was a nation closed to America and its citizens, a nation with whom we were effectively at war. Viewing China from Hong Kong's terminal train station seemed as close to this mystical ruler of the Orient as we would ever get in our lives.

As we described our plans to Mr. Fink shortly after breakfast that morning he protested. "You don't want the train. You need a car, a guide," he insisted.

"That's not in our budget," Joanne and I protested.

"Ah, but it is in mine. And I want you to dine with Madame Zhou and me tonight. Don't worry," he added, his eyes twinkling in glee, "I won't keep you so long you can't go dancing afterward."

Before we knew it, our short, balding, Jewish Santa had ordered a car complete with a young driver to take Joanne and me on our own personal tour of Hong Kong.

Our driver was a 25-year old Chinese man who called himself Tony. A refugee from mainland China, Tony was eager to show us Hong Cong. He spoke excellent English, and was our perfect tour guide.

Maneuvering a small limousine through Old Hong Kong's crowded streets Tony took us to see the most elegant of all the British Clubs in the city. We ate a picnic lunch on the beach near a traditional Chinese fishing village, watching the sampans maneuver in and out of the coastal waters. From there we could see the island of Macao floating distantly on the water like one more sampan.

He took us to see an ancient walled village, long protected from the modern world by its high fortification. Stepping inside was like stepping back a millennium. He took us through the new territories where we saw high rise upon high rise apartment building, teeming

Joanne and Mr. Fink in front of the Hong Kong Peninsula

with people, in this bustling city of six million crammed into a few square miles of territory jointly owned by Britain and China.

And finally, he took us to the northern most hill in Hong Kong, as close to the Chinese border as he dared drive the car. From our vantage, on Hong Kong's highest hill, we could see Communist China below. Irrigated rice patties, separated one from another by small stands of trees, stretched out toward the horizon. From our hilltop vista China looked no different than any other landscape in Southeast Asia.

That night, we found ourselves, attired in our best dresses and new jewelry, sitting across from Mr. Fink and Madame Zhou while he explained the nature of their business dealings.

Through years of business transactions they'd become good friends. After describing her company Madame Zhou formally presented each of us with one of her factory's newest products, a long rectangular carry-on bag that could be stretched and pulled to carry an entire week's worth of essentials. Mr. Fink nudged her, and she produced yet another carry-on, this one in canvas.

As soon as she was able, Madame Zhou excused herself. Mr.

Fink soon followed, but not before he added the dinner to his ever-burgeoning tab. We finished eating in quiet contentment, commenting on how good it felt to be dressed in real clothes, to wear make-up and high heels.

After dinner we took the ferry to the main island to check out the action at The Hong Kong Hilton. The hotel was stunningly modern and attractive. One of the ballrooms was filled with dancing GIs who wanted to leave the War behind as much as we did. Perhaps because we were officers, perhaps because we were just a little bit older, perhaps because we were not looking to get laid, we felt out of place. How lucky we were to be at the Peninsula!

On Thursday morning, Joanne, Carolyn, and I decided we had no choice but to face an unwanted task. The packages we had delivered to the Peninsula on Monday now had to be returned to the Base Exchange so that we could ship them to Vietnam using the US Postal Service. Why hadn't we figured this out before? We had so much to transfer across part of Hong Kong's deep bay we decided we needed to rent a car for an hour or two.

Our limousine driver was young Tony, our friend from the previous day. With absolute ease, he carried box upon box from the hotel to the car and then from the car to the post office inside the Base Exchange. Grateful, we tried to dismiss him with a big tip. He would not leave. Instead, he insisted on staying until we had paid for the last package to be sent on its way to Vietnam.

Joanne hit upon the idea of thanking Tony by taking him out to dinner that night. We dismissed the floating restaurant after Carolyn developed a mild case of traveler's revenge, contracted while dining with her friend from the Royal Navy. We had already eaten three elegantly prepared meals at the Peninsula, and doubted that management would look favorably upon an employee dining with guests in one of its fine restaurants.

Instead so we chose a small restaurant, reputed to have the best French food in all of Hong Kong. I ate French onion soup for the first time, returning most of the hearty broth to the bowl as I unsuccessfully tried time after time to fill my spoon with a bit of soup, a bit of crouton, and a bit of melted gruyere. The four of us laughed, and laughed certain I would starve.

As we talked as we realized the differences between our cultures were less important than the commonalities that bound us. Why couldn't our leaders in Washington or Peking see that?

On Sunday morning we found Mr. Fink, sitting with his newspaper, drinking coffee and eating a scone. We offered our most sincere thanks to our new friend for the extraordinary kindness he had shown us over the preceding six days. He told us to keep safe. Then we returned to our room to sink ourselves into that bathtub one last time.

By noon we had shrugged off our ball gowns, thrown out our glass slippers, and put on our dress greens. Our Cinderella week in Hong Kong as guests of the most unlikely prince an Army nurse could imagine was over. We boarded our flying pumpkin and returned to the war.

Chapter 26.
WELCOME TO WARD 1

That first morning back from my fairy-tale like stay in Hong Kong, I reported for duty on Ward 1, where I found myself being oriented to the Ward's routines by Carol, a fellow Pennsylvanian who lived next to Carol Ann in Hooch 4. Carol and I had grown up about 15 miles from each other, and attended rival high schools. Although we were the same age, and had graduated from high school the same year, she had gone to a three-year hospital school of nursing, and thus had been in the Army Nurse Corps a year longer than I.

Things were quiet that day. We had no patients. So Carol had plenty of time to orient me to my new workplace and its routines.

The physical layout of Ward 1 was different from the hospital's other wards. To the right of the ward's entrance from the emergency room were five or six twin sets of saw horses. Two saw horses, spaced about four feet apart, could hold a stretcher carrying a 200-pound man. This was the preoperative staging area for men waiting to go into the OR. An extension of the Emergency Room, this part of Ward 1, was "blood and guts." Placing a privacy screen around an *expectant* patient happened more often here, and the work was intense. The men awaiting their turn in the OR needed constant monitoring to assure us their condition was stable.

To the left of the ER entrance to Ward 1 was the nurses' station and the post-operative recovery area. Patients left Ward 1 for the OR on stretchers. They returned in regular hospital beds, with the areas around their wounds thoroughly cleansed, and incisions or open areas covered in layers of gauze bandage. Our job on this side

Dec, 1970: Me in front of Ward 1

of the Ward was much like that of any other Recovery Room.

Once patients could be awakened from anesthesia the corpsmen bathed them. No one was ever sent to the receiving ward dirty. In the five months I was on Ward 1 I lost count of the number of patients whose fingers were dipped in hot, soapy water while diligent corpsmen worked hard to remove dirt from under their fingernails and between their toes. I thought Brunhilda needed to come by to assist with one of these baths. But she never did.

There were always two nurses and at least two corpsmen assigned to Ward 1: one each for pre-op, the other for post-op. How busy we were depended entirely on the number of patients coming into the 24th Evac. Some days—or nights—we barely sat down. Other days we had lots of free time on our hand.

When things were quiet—a word we hated to utter aloud in case we jinxed ourselves— we spent time visiting the ER, lab, and x-ray. Anything to look busy: we hated the idea of being asked to spend the night helping on one of the in-patient surgical wards. Unfamiliar with another ward's set-up we were mostly left alone.

On Ward 5, Ted encouraged us to go to our hooches during

the night to take naps if the census allowed. On Ward 1 people sometimes slept at the nurses' station, their head propped between their arms.

I was never comfortable with this, and, if I had a good book, rarely struggled to stay awake on slow nights. By then my sister Laura had graduated from college and become engaged to her husband Larry, then a senior at Yale. On Laura's first visits to Yale to see Larry she sat in on a popular English professor's class. The professor was Erich Segal whose book "Love Story" had just become a runaway best seller. Laura sent me a copy, telling me I would love it. One boring night I read it cover to cover during my 12-hour shift. I thanked Laura profusely, and lent the book to my fellow nurses, where it quickly became a prized read. But, frankly, I thought it was stupid. Was it the book or me? Probably a little bit of both, for I certainly was developing a more and more jaundiced view of the world.

Although I easily made friends with the other nurses and corpsmen, the only person with whom I developed a lasting friendship was Carol. Sometimes I missed Ward 5: the easy camaraderie that had grown between nurses and corpsmen, despite, or perhaps because of, the intensity of patient care. With more than half my tour of duty over, I had plenty of friends with whom I could socialize during my off-duty hours. Ward 1 was all about intense nursing without getting to know the patients— exactly what I wanted.

Being on Ward 1 also afforded me the opportunity to get to know COL Stuart Roberts, MD who had been Chief of Surgery at Ohio State University, before taking a sabbatical to study the relationship between time of injury and that of receiving care in an emergency room or aid station. Although it seemed self-evident that the sooner a wounded man could get to the hospital, the better the outcome, Dr. Roberts especially wanted to determine the role the routine use of specially equipped helicopters played in patient survival.

As Chief of Surgery for Vietnam Stuart could have commandeered a "luxury suite" near MACV Headquarters. This was not what he wanted—it was too far from the action. Instead he lived in a comfortably furnished two room, air-conditioned hooch a short walk from the back door of our Hooch 3.

During his time in Vietnam Stuart made friends with several of the nurses in the surgical ICU, included Joanne and Stephanie. It was not unusual for them—or the three of us—to visit with Stuart for an hour or so, whenever he wasn't visiting another hospital or battalion aid station.

It was a delight to hear him talk about home and his family, and enlightening to listen to him talk about both the history of the helicopter and its use in evacuating the wounded—for Stuart had a keen interest in helicopters. He had met Igor Sikorsky, a Russian immigrant to the United States who had developed the rotor system used by modern helicopters.

Living on the grounds of the 24th Evac, and three miles from both the 93rd Evac and the 45th (Dustoff) Air Ambulance Medical Unit afforded Stuart the opportunity to easily fly wherever he wanted to go, even if it put him in harm's way. Dustoff pilots sometimes hesitated to take Dr. Roberts to a potentially unsafe landing zone, but he was well aware of the risks, and gladly took them.

Chapter 27.

FIRST, DO NO HARM

Everyone who worked at the 24th Evac had an opinion about the surgery. We were evenly divided between those who believed the neurosurgeons were recklessly taking unnecessary risks to perform a complicated, elective procedure on an uninjured child, and those who believed the surgery would not only give the child a new lease on life but would also be an important gesture of goodwill.

The doctors involved would never have considered the surgery if things hadn't been unusually slow. But the casualty rate was down and the doctors were bored. Things were so slow at the 24th Evac—not that we were complaining—that, once again, we increased our humanitarian outreach programs to the civilian population.

And so, when General Cho* and his wife brought their only child, a 12-year-old boy, to the hospital for treatment of severe scoliosis the doctors began to talk about surgery. It was almost certain that young Banh would not be able to grow normally without constant corrective bracing: both expensive and difficult to find in his third world country with its third world health care system. There was one hope for him to live a near normal life: surgery to correct the twists in his spinal column.

Although the 24th Evac had the most modern and well equipped surgical suites of any hospital in Vietnam the risks were enormous. It was a long and delicate procedure, not the kind of thing to take lightly under any circumstance, and certainly not in a war zone. Providing proper anesthesia and fluid replacement would be paramount. Too little fluid and the child could die of hypovolemic shock; too much could cause swelling, dangerously pressing Bahn's delicate spinal cord against the very structures meant to protect it. And then there was the ever-present risk of infection. The arguments for and against the surgery swirled through the hospital for days, until Stuart Roberts got involved. In disputes of this nature he had the final say.

At first Stuart vetoed the surgery, but the boy's parents were persistent. They wanted Banh to have the procedure. Their vision of their son's future without the surgery was dismal: he would be crippled by age thirty, dying of pneumonia or some other complication. They had absolute trust that the American doctors could save their son.

The surgeons hand-picked the OR crew for Banh's surgery. The chief of anesthesia would put him to sleep and watch over every drop of Lactated Ringers solution to drip into his veins. The OR nurses would have the deftest fingers, able to hold forceps and needles just so while the surgeons did their job.

I do not know, will never know, why or if I was selected to be Banh's nurse in the recovery room. I had only been a nurse for 14 months, but had been in Vietnam half that time. I had spent six months working on the neurosurgical intensive care unit, and only had recently transferred to Ward 1. Perhaps the doctors thought highly of my ability to recognize problems and act on them. Perhaps they thought my recent experience on the neuro-ICU would be of benefit. Perhaps they gave no consideration whatsoever to the fact that once the surgery was over they would be entrusting their young patient to a relatively inexperienced nurse.

Activity on Ward 1 was quiet that day, as if the fighting was temporarily suspended while the doctors operated on this little boy. Periodic reports from the OR indicated the surgery was going well, though more slowly than expected.

Around 1500 hours someone from the OR came out to tell me that they were closing the surgical incision. Banh would soon be entrusted into my care. The surgery had lasted more than seven

———

*Names have been changed.

hours, much longer than anticipated.

Moments later Derek Jennison, the anesthesiologist, and an OR nurse wheeled Banh's bed from the operating room into the recovery area. As the surgical nurse gave her report I did my initial assessment. Before me lay a small, thin boy with silky black hair peeking out from under a surgical cap. His skin was the color of pale amber, normal, I thought for a child of Asian heritage. Out of habit I pressed my finger into the skin of his small right foot. The capillary refill, which indicates sufficient flow of blood to the extremities, and thus is a measure of hydration, seemed adequate.

Bahn lay on his now straight back, which was covered with a thick dressing made of several layers of gauze sealed in adhesive tape. It was dry and intact. Dark yellow urine trickled from a foley catheter into a bag attached to the stretcher frame. A pliant plastic IV needle gave access to a vein and through this the Ringers dripped slowly. He was naked, covered only by a ceil blue sheet. I counted his pulse and respirations, took a blood pressure and a rectal temp. All were normal. There was every indication that Banh would wake up soon and begin recovery toward a healthier life.

Next, I listened carefully as Jennison gave his detailed instructions about the specifics of Banh's postoperative care. Of utmost importance would be the timing of the IV. I had a pediatric IV set primed with a mere 50cc of Ringers ready to hang.

I did the first three sets of vital signs and saw nothing to cause alarm. Then Banh began to wake up. He seemed unusually agitated even for a child. I called Jennison. Was his agitation likely to disturb the surgical repair? He assured me it would not, and reminded me to keep the IV running at 50 ccs/hour.

Just then a senior nurse anesthetist walked past. She took one look at Banh and yelled for me to come quickly to the bedside.

"Get Jennison here right now," she pronounced, as she reached up and twisted the IV stopcock to its wide-open position, allowing the solution to flow freely into Banh's vein.

"What?" I began to ask, "...are you doing?" I never finished the sentence.

"This isn't agitation from anesthesia; this is air hunger. This kid is about to arrest." Before she could say another word Banh stopped breathing.

She began external chest massage while I hit the big red emergency button that alerted the ER we needed help. An ER doctor arrived less than a minute later. He took over the chest massage while the anesthetist attached tubing from one of the oxygen tanks to an ambu bag and began forcing highly concentrated oxygen into Banh's lungs. I took on the role of recorder, while someone got supplies.

Dr Jennison arrived, his face pale, his features grim. He began pumping on Banh's thin chest, trading off with the ER doctor. Someone mixed the appropriate concentration of epinephrine and injected it through Banh's chest into his heart. It didn't work. There was still no heartbeat.

After about an hour someone suggested that we "call the code." Jennison refused. His bleak stare spoke volumes: this is all my fault. I have to save this child.

"Can somebody find Ralph Sievers please?" A corpsman raced to the phone. But before he had a chance to dial the number to Ralph's hooch, the thoracic surgeon appeared, accompanied by Dr Roberts.

After a hasty discussion, which I barely had time to note, I watched the doctors hurriedly cover themselves in masks, surgical gowns and hats before donning sterile gloves. Someone threw me a mask and told me to put it on. I continued to write, scribbling as quickly as I could.

Ralph opened a sterile packet of surgical instruments and quickly cut into the correct space between Bahn's frail ribs. He enlarged the incision until he could see Banh's heart. He cradled the muscle in his strong, skilled hands and began to squeeze and then release. "One and two and three and," he began counting rhythmically out loud. Blood seeped out of Banh's chest cavity, covering the front of Ralph's gown. Dr. Roberts pushed Ralph's hands out of the way and injected yet another dose of epinephrine into the muscle. Banh's heart still did not beat. Ralph began squeezing methodically again.

After an hour of continuous direct cardiac massage he looked despairingly at Derek Jennison.

"OK," Jennison said. Ralph stopped squeezing. Someone looked at the wall clock and pronounced, "Time of death 1714."

No one spoke as Ralph replaced Banh's small, still heart into his small, still chest. With a practiced hand, he closed the chest incision. A corpsman cleaned up the now blood-soaked floor. Someone else washed the blood from Banh's body, picked him up tenderly and placed him on a clean bed, covering him with a sheet.

Then Dr Jennison led the parents into the room, its bright overhead lights gleaming on the harsh reality of a day gone terribly wrong, a life lost, and Banh's mother's softly keening wails.

The nurse anesthetist sat at the nurses' station, her face set in a stony mix of anger and frustration.

"Did I..." I began, but could not continue. "Should I have..." I tried again.

"No, Lieutenant, you are not responsible for this. Apart from the fact we should not have done the surgery, this child died of hypovolemia. They probably underestimated blood loss during the surgery."

Finally, Jennison led the grieving parents out the door. Bahn and I were alone in 1. I put my head down on the desk and wept.

Chapter 28.
LIEUTENANT JOHN DOE

When he first arrived at 24th Evac, no one knew the young soldier's name, only his rank.

The exploding mortar shell that blew off his dog tags and most of his uniform left only a few tattered shreds from which we could see a bar of burnished gold and black embroidered onto a frayed collar, making him a Second Lieutenant. LT John Doe. His platoon had taken a serious hit and was in disarray, the number of casualties unknown, with no one available to identify the dead or wounded.

The shell's force had rattled the young Lieutenant's head with such power he was in a deep coma, unresponsive to pain, his pupils fixed and dilated—a sign of brain death. The explosion collapsed both lungs, shattered both legs and arms, and the heat of it seared his face and neck. No one expected him to live.

Protocols for caring for patients, developed first in WWII, then in Korea, before being refined in Vietnam, deemed that patients with minor wounds, who could be treated and returned to battle should be cared for first. The remaining, more seriously wounded patients were either *expected* (as in the patient is expected to live) or *expectant*, a cruel grammatical play on words meaning the patient was expected to die. *Expected* patients received secondary priority for treatment. *Expectant patients were last.* No one ever liked declaring a patient *expectant*— something only the doctors could do—and when we did, we hoped he would survive until the operating rooms were free and we could treat him the same as we would treat any other patient.

Overwhelmed by patients that afternoon the ER doctors made the dreadful decision to declare LT John Doe *expectant*, then shipped him to the neuro-ICU to die.

When I got to work that night LT John Doe lay near the front of the unit, his bed surrounded by screens to give his dying the privacy it deserved.

"Is that what I think it is?" I pointed in John Doe's direction.

"Yup," my friend and co-worker Carol Ann replied.

"Shit." It was my last rotation of nights before going to Hong Kong on leave. When I returned I would begin a new assignment on Ward 1. I had hoped for a quiet night, during which I might get to chat with my fellow nurses, or even take a brief nap, but it didn't look as though the War was going to let that happen.

"Don't worry, he won't be with us much longer," Carol Ann said.

"How long does he have?" I was not asking Carol Ann to guess how soon LT John Doe would die. Rather I wanted to know how long he had been at the 24th Evac. Maybe, just maybe, he would live long enough for the OR to be cleared of patients.

"Oh, I don't know maybe five hours," Carol Ann said.

Lt John Doe lay behind the screen, covered only by a sheet, a naked, bloodied mess. The ER staff had cut off the remaining shreds of his uniform, searching for wounds. They'd inserted chest tubes and a tracheotomy to make it easier for him to breathe, and covered his remaining wounds as best they could. Old, dried blood, some of it thick as gauze, covered John Doe's trunk and both legs. At least the fractures of his leg bones had not pierced his skin.

Around midnight someone from admitting arrived, bearing LT John Doe's real name, and with it the information that his father was a Brigadier General. The Army had already notified John Doe's father of his son's serious wounds, and he, knowing the ways of the Army, had made a somewhat unusual request: could we try to keep his son alive until he could get to Vietnam to say good-bye?

The General was pulling rank, and we all knew it. To honor it we would have to open our reserve operating room, rouse more OR nurses from their beds, and free up a surgeon to operate on the young Lieutenant. It was a risk the doctors chose to take, and not because John Doe's father was a General. Rather it was the vision each of us had developed on some level during their year: of a military officer—accompanied by a chaplain—standing at a family's front door greeting them with their most dreadful news. That this scene was played out hundreds of times a day across the country was not something we allowed ourselves to think about. Honoring the General's request gave us a chance to make peace with our inability to save all for whom we cared. And so, for the father's sake, not the wounded son's, the doctors decided to try save the young man's life. Within the hour two corpsmen wheeled the dying patient to the operating room. When I left work that morning he was still in surgery.

I slept until dinnertime, got up, took a shower, dressed in fatigues and combat boots and headed to the mess hall for dinner. Promptly at 1845 I reported for duty.

As I checked my mailbox I saw my favorite corpsman, Zak. "What happened to that expectant guy from last night?" I asked.

"He's still here."

"He survived the surgery?"

"Yep," Zak replied. "I hear they want to air evac him to Japan tomorrow."

"How in the hell are they going to manage that?" I was astounded, knowing it normally took more than a week to stabilize someone as sick as John Doe for the long flight to Japan. If he didn't die first.

"They're going to send him with his own doc," Zak shook his head as if to say *what a waste*, then added, "Guess his Dad's pulled some serious rank. Oh yeah, it's that new jerk of an ER doc they're sending with him."

When I arrived for work the following evening Lt John Doe had just left. A mixed blessing, we rarely knew what happened to our patients after they left the 24th Evac. It was better that way. John Doe was just another kid who had briefly touched our lives. We did not think he would survive and did not expect to hear anything about him again. But we were wrong.

Chapter 29.
ROMANCES

When Stuart Roberts arrived in Vietnam his purpose was to study the use of helicopters during rescue missions. It turned out he had another role: match-maker.

One night after I'd transferred to Ward 1, I heard Dr Roberts poking through the record room, which was housed in a space between the ER and Ward 1. We had no patients and I was bored. I wandered into the record room, offering to help.

While we pulled and reviewed charts, Stuart casually mentioned his budding friendship with a First Cav Med-Evac pilot, Monty Halcomb. Did I think Joanne would be interested in dating this handsome young pilot with sandy hair and an impressive mustache?

"Nothing lost in asking," I responded, though what I really wanted to say was, "What about me? I think I might be interested."

Joanne Kane was kind, caring, and beautiful. Monty Halcomb was dashingly handsome, funny, and adventurous. The attraction was immediate and intense. Four months after we left Vietnam I traveled to New York where I was maid of honor and Stuart Roberts was best man at the wedding of Joanne Kane and Monty Halcomb.

Theirs may have seemed like a dangerously short courtship, especially by today's standards. But being in a war changes many things. And knowing when one should get married, and to whom, was among them. Living with constant danger and its aftermath matured us in a way our friends from home had not experienced. Monty had survived flying into dangerous landing zones in a helicopter—a relatively unsafe flying machine in relation to fixed wing aircraft. Joanne had lost count of the number of men who died in her care.

Their courtship was not unusual. Ward 7 nurse Mary Reynolds, who arrived in Vietnam in November, met her husband Dr Doug Powell in Vietnam. A fellow Ward 5 nurse and one of our corpsmen fell in love in Vietnam and married as soon as they got home. I have seen both Tom and Bev at a 24th Evac reunion. They have been married for 46 years. Decades later I met a fellow writer who had been at the 12th Evac in 1969. She met her husband there; the two married as soon as they got back to the States, then joined the Peace Corps together.

However, there is no question that that when it comes to love stories with happy endings despite the war, nothing could beat that of my Ward 1 pal, Carol Konieczny and Larry Brown. They were married in the hospital chapel the day after Thanksgiving, November 28, 1970.

Carol was from Western Pennsylvania, Larry from Oregon. They were already engaged when they received orders for Vietnam. Both had large, extended families who wanted the wedding on their home turf. If ever there was an engaged couple in need of a destination wedding it was Carol and Larry. And so, they decided to marry in Vietnam.

Thanksgiving 26 Nov 1970
24th Evac

Wedding Kiss

Larry & Carol Konieczny Brown Wedding Day on 28 November 1970

Civil wedding done

Cutting the cake

Carol, Larry, & Mike

When she arrived in country, Carol brought with her a simple, elegant knee length white dress and a veil. I thought she was joking about getting married in Vietnam until she showed me the dress.

It took months to cut through the red tape necessary for Carol and Larry to wed. Carol even had to swear she would not get pregnant during the rest of her stay in country. They asked for leave and got it, beginning the day after Thanksgiving.

While most brides primp and preen on the day before their wedding Carol did what she always did: she went to work on Ward 1. She, Carol Ann, another Ward 5 nurse, and I ate Thanksgiving dinner together that afternoon.

The next day, while trying to remove some wrinkles from her veil Carol scorched it. Some of the resourceful seamstresses among us were able to remove the scorched spot by shortening the veil. It may have been one of the shortest veils ever, but it was still attractive. The reception, attended by everyone not on duty filled the Officer's Club.

Chapter 30.
CHRISTMAS EVE

No more than 100 feet above ground, the helicopter skimmed over the lush, green jungle. Monty Halcomb was flying left seat. His copilot Tom—"T"—was flying right seat. In the back of the Bell UH1H "Huey" helicopter a gunner sat at each door, eyes raking the Vietnamese landscape, prepared to use the machine guns mounted onto the helicopter's floor. As we flew, I sat on the floor next to the door gunner, holding onto the frame, kicking my legs over the side like a little girl on a porch swing instead of what I was —a nurse taking an illegal ride on a medical evacuation helicopter.

Riding along with us were two medics, and Stephanie and Joanne. We were on a mission of great importance. No, we were not rescuing wounded or taking them to hospital. It was December 24th and we were looking for something we could turn into a Christmas tree.

The jungle below thinned out and an abandoned rubber plantation came into view. We swooped down over the ruined mansion, saw a swimming pool filled with water the color of French onion soup. A rubber tree would not do. We flew on.

We had been in the air about an hour, touching down and failing twice to find the right tree, before T and Monty decided we would have to make do with whatever we could find in the next ten minutes. T eased back on the stick, the whine of the rotors changing pitch as we sunk down until the helicopter hovered six feet off the ground. Beside us was a small stand of trees. The two corpsmen jumped from the helicopter and began their search. My heart pounded, my whitening knuckles still grasping the door frame as I watched them go from tree to tree. This was taking way too long. Maybe I transmitted my anxiety telepathically for they finally fixed on a tree the deep green of a North American Pine, quickly cut it down, and tossed it into the back of the chopper.

It was a more like a holly bush than a tree, and although it bore no red berries it had something else in common with a holly bush: its leaves ended in points sharp enough to prick the skin. We discovered this almost as soon as we got the thing on board the helicopter. But we had already been too long in the air. Time to get it home.

For Monty, T, and their crew, home was a desolate square of wooden buildings, sand bags, asphalt landing zones, and dozens of helicopters of various makes and models surrounded by rows of concertina wire reaching 15 feet into the air. This was Fire Base Mace, an outpost of the First Cavalry, Air Mobile. To build Fire Base Mace the First Cav had had to destroy a once luxurious carpet of native foliage, exposing the rust colored Vietnamese soil. In the rainy season, the place turned to mud, a brick maker's dream. But in the dry season, as it was now, the soil turned to pulverized cinnamon, whipped up from the ground by the helicopter's rotor's like a Mixmaster whirling over a plate of red flour. It got in your hair, up your nose, down your bra, in the creases behind your knees. I had stopped wearing contact lenses because of the dust.

We reached the hooch Monty and T shared with a couple of other pilots. The tree soon followed. Someone nailed the trunk onto a base, found the lights, and began to wrap them around the tree.

"Fuck."

A collective, "What?"

"This damn tree is infested with ants." There were, in fact, thousands of them. My ingenuous pilot friends dragged the tree outside, found a hose, and sprayed it down with water, the ants scurrying away as we tromped on them with our combat boots, creating miniature red clouds as we stomped. The tree glistened in the afternoon sun. All it needed was a little snow. OK, it also needed cones, needles, and the scent of pine resin instead of the odor that wafted in the air. Burning shit. What else?

We took the tree inside, strung the lights, and hung the decorations, most of which were silvery and khaki circles fashioned

*Standing by a Cobra "attack" helicopter on Christmas Eve.
I chickened out when offered a ride.*

*Monty, Joanne, and the gang
Fire Base Mace, Christmas Eve, 1970*

from c-ration cans. Someone had found a box of tinsel in Saigon that we threw at the bush with the enthusiasm of eight-year olds allowed to help decorate the family tree for the first time. T plugged the lights into a wall socket and the colored lights twinkled. We stood in the dim light filtering through the hooch's front door and admired our handiwork.

We had all brought food from care packages and would, in good time, make ourselves a feast of canned Polish Ham, baby sausages, fudge, Christmas cookies, and fruitcake.

But first to enjoy the moment. We scaled the sandbags rimming Monty's hooch and sat on the roof. Someone broke out the beer. Christmas carols floated through loudspeakers. We drank cool liquid as the sun darkened to burnished gold. It was Vietnam, and it was Christmas. And we forgot we were in a war.

Chapter 31.

LEAVIN' ON A JET PLANE

I was short. My DEROS calendar was almost completely colored in. I already had orders to report to Ireland Army Hospital at Ft Knox, KY on 17 March. Rather than go straight home I had asked for a flight to Japan. Having received a second back payment for the months I should have been a Captain, I had the money to spend. Although I was desperate to see my family, I never expected to return to the Orient; I wanted to see a little of Japan before I left the Far East.

As the first of our group to arrive in Vietnam I was also the first to leave. I would claim an apartment in the nurses' quarters at Ft Knox to share with Carol Ann after she arrived. Joanne and Monty had orders for Ft Lewis, Washington. Susan and Stephanie still had months left in Vietnam. Neither had an idea where she would be sent next.

My orders put me on a flight out of Saigon on Saturday 13 February 1971. That morning I was up early, eager to leave. My meager belongings were already on their way home. I had a few clothes, a new stereo system, and some books. What I had to carry home were a change of civilian clothing and white nurse's uniforms in case my belongings did not arrive at Ft Knox before I did. The plaster Buddha that had been in my room when I arrived and the small doll my sister Susie had given me when I left home both crumbled in my fingers when I was packing. They went into the trash along with my jungle fatigues and combat boots.

I only wanted my boonies hat and dog tags to remind me of the year. The hat had Captain's bars, a 24th Evac insignia pin and another from the First Cav. What else did I need?

Hugging my friends good-bye, I walked to the administration building, where I would be picked up for the trip to Saigon. My chariot was late. Growing more anxious and excited by the moment I decided to pee one last time. I walked back to my hooch to use the bathroom. Once inside, I could hear someone's radio playing the AFVN station. The song was Peter, Paul, and Mary's *Jet Plane*.

As I walked back to the administration building I saw no one. I could feel the rhythm of the hospital's day unfolding, but I was no longer a part of it. It was as though the earth had opened and swallowed me. The war was beating inexorably on, but I was no longer needed. I was going home.

Five days later, on Thursday 18 February 1971, exactly one year to the day after my flight soared over the Pacific en route to Vietnam, I stood in the terminal of the Greater Pittsburgh Airport, hugging my family. We were all crying. Our tears were of relief mixed with joy.

Over the weekend I listened to my sister Laura, 15 months my junior and a newly minted music teacher, tell me of meeting Erich Segal, whose book she had sent me while I was in Vietnam. Now she regaled me with the story of sitting in on one of his classes with her fiancé Larry, who was a senior at Yale. We laughed at her stories of going to Yale the first time, where she met Larry's suite mates, including a pre-med student named Howard Dean. [Yes, that Howard Dean.]

I dredged my memory banks for acceptable stories, telling Laura about purple alerts, going to Vung Tau, spending Christmas Eve at Fire Base Mace. Of my parents' four daughters, Laura was the only one not destined to become a nurse. She disliked doctors and all things medical and didn't understand how I could be fascinated by the things she found revolting.

We joked I could not be a music teacher like her because I had no rhythm. I did not tell her she could not have withstood Vietnam. I did not think anyone in my family, except possibly my dad, whose stories of pulling burning airmen from wrecked bombers during WWII, had helped me decide against the 93rd Evac, could understand the blood and brutality I had witnessed.

A week after I came home, my mother and I went to Greensburg's largest department store in search of some new clothes for me. While we were there we ran into one of my friends from elementary school.

"Barbie, you're home!" Linda pulled me close for a hug. Then she held me at arms' length like a long-lost aunt inspecting her niece. "How was it?"

I took a deep breath, trying to find a few words that would describe what I had just been through. Before I could compose a single sentence, she rattled on, "Oh let me tell you about the cute guy I just met."

That was Linda. But her response was typical. Even close friends were not particularly interested in what I had been through. I couldn't tell the people closest to me, especially my parents, what it had really been like. They were proud I had gone to war. I could not disabuse them of their heartfelt belief that I had done something noble.

Chapter 32.

THE REUNION

In July 1993, the 24th Evac held a reunion at the Mayflower Hotel in Washington, DC. Many of my friends were there, including Carol, Carol Ann, Valerie, Susan, and Stephanie. There were few corpsmen there. No Zak or Howie. Most of the people at the reunion were doctors, nurses, and Medical Service Corps officers and their spouses. We renewed old acquaintances, and struck up new ones. But we did not focus on what we had done during the war. Rather we talked about our current lives. Carol was the Chief Nurse of the Oregon National Guard. Larry, still sporting a fabulous looking handle bar mustache, was with her.

The head nurse on Ward 1, Diane Corcoran had become one of nursing's premiere experts on near death experiences—an interest she developed from being in Vietnam. She and I spent a lot of time deep in conversation because I had developed the same interest over my own nursing career.

Valerie and Susan had stayed in the Army and were both still on active duty. Susan, who lived outside D.C., was married to a Marine Corps Fighter Pilot and had three children. But Valerie and her husband were divorced. Stephanie was working in a hospital in Mississippi; Carol Ann, now held a PhD in Psychology, and taught nursing in Chicago. I had taught maternal-child nursing and was working as a staff nurse in a small maternity unit at the local hospital in my picturesque New England town. Even Nora Hoffmann was there. She didn't remember our brief encounter in Vietnam, but did remember me from our days on the school bus. The only one of my

L to R: Myself, Valerie, Carol Ann, July 1993.

close friends to be absent from the reunion was Joanne.

The Vietnam Women's Memorial would be dedicated in four months, its construction on The Mall, in a small stand of trees across from The Wall was already underway. The bronze statue of three women dressed in fatigues was not yet in place. But Carol Ann, Valerie, and I still walked from the hotel to the Memorial for a sneak preview. A monument in Washington, D.C. dedicated to us. Fabulous!

Amazingly, some of our former patients were at the reunion, too. Among them was a man about our age whose face bore the residual effect of second degree burns. He walked with a cane, but otherwise seemed to have suffered no serious, long-term effects from whatever injuries he sustained in Vietnam.

As we got reacquainted we quickly learned that this former patient had a fantastic story to tell: he had been declared *expectant*, but survived. Told he would be unable to live a normal life and would never walk again he had defied everyone's expectations. For he was married and the father of three, and worked as a senior administrator in a Veterans' Administration Hospital in Virginia. He had come to the reunion specifically to thank us for saving his life.

At the banquet on the final night of the reunion, participants were invited to speak, sharing their memories of the year in our hell. Most of those who spoke were doctors, explaining how their time in Vietnam had influenced their careers.

Then one of the former ER doctors stood, and in a long, rambling speech, described how angry he had been at being assigned to the ER instead of becoming the ENT specialist for which he had been receiving training when he was drafted. The highlight of his year had been the time he was asked to accompany a severely wounded patient to Japan.

Then the man with the cane limped to the podium. "I believe I am the patient you accompanied to Japan," he said. "I doubt if you would remember my name, but you might remember my story. I was wounded in September 1970. You called me LT John Doe. You didn't let me die because my Dad was a General. I am here to thank you for saving my life."

As one, we stood and applauded.

POST SCRIPT

I retired from nursing at the end of May 2009, a few days after I celebrated my 62nd birthday. Like most people, I envisioned myself working—at least part time—until I turned sixty-five. But life, as it always does, had other plans. My mother, then in her late eighties, had moved to nearby Kittery, Maine; I willingly became the daughter who helped her meet her needs, whether it was grocery shopping, going to the bank, or visiting her internist. My daughter Karen had a two-year old daughter, Alice. In coordination with her other grandparents, Jim and I took turns watching Alice whenever both parents' work schedule required our help.

At work, I was both respected and overlooked by my fellow nurses in their twenties and thirties, all outstanding nurses who seemed unable to grasp that I might arrive at work with graying hair, but had been working in maternal-child nursing before some of them were born.

One night, two years before I retired, I had tripped over the ten-pound weight we used to calibrate our baby scale, a weight we also used to hold a pesky door open. When I tripped, I flew across the hallway, landing against the far hall with my right shoulder—without dropping the medication I was taking to one of my patients! The follow-up x-rays of my shoulder proved what I had long suspected, that I had inherited my mother's severe osteoarthritis, and that my shoulders were already filled with arthritic bone spurs and cysts. Much as I loved being a labor nurse I had reached a point where allowing laboring mothers to push against my body simply made my own physical ailments worse.

At sixty-two, I was a young retiree. What to do with my time? My husband, who had retired two years earlier, pointed out I could do anything I wanted, within reason. No, I couldn't become a talented cellist like Yo Yo Ma, nor was it likely I could become the next P.D. James or Diana Gabaldon, two of my favorite writers, but I now had the time I needed in which to write.

And so, almost exactly forty years from the day my old instructor inspired my epiphany I began to write, thanks to the writing programs at the Osher Life Long Learning Institute (OLLI) in conjunction with the University of Southern Maine.

My first instructor was Ruth Townsend Story; my first classmates included Nancy Freund Bills, and Joan Kost. Together these three women helped me discover that, indeed, I could write. When I joined them in a monthly writers' workshop, they encouraged me to write—and keep writing—about Vietnam. I will forever be in their debt for believing in me—and for encouraging me to write the hard parts, particularly the chapter we all referred to as the *Sex, Drugs, and Rock 'n Roll* chapter. Tom Holbrook of Piscataqua Press, publisher of "When I Die," took a chance on me early in his endeavors to establish a small publishing house in conjunction with Portsmouth, New Hampshire's excellent bookstore, RiverRun.

So now, as we approach, or have already crossed the bridge to our seventieth birthdays where are we? Carol and Larry Brown live in Oregon. They have two sons and several grandchildren, and usually drive to interesting places to visit with friends. Carol spent much of her career as the senior medical officer of the Oregon National Guard.

Carol Ann Rogers, divorced from her first husband, recently married Mark, her sweetheart of many years. A month after the wedding her daughter threw Carol Ann and Mark a wedding reception; I was delighted to be able to attend it.

Joanne and Monty live in Southeastern Tennessee, where they own a small farm. Both are involved in their church. Monty enjoys hunting, donating venison and other wild meats to people in need. Joanne loves tending to her horses. They have two children, both about the same age as my two oldest. We saw each other last in 2014, and spent so many hours talking and laughing Monty asked us if he needed to pipe extra oxygen into the room where we sat.

*Carol & Larry Brown renewal of Wedding vows 28 Nov 2005
Notre Dame Cathedral Seigon Vietnam*

In 2014 the 24th Evac held another reunion in Branson, MO. Joanne and I drove from her home to Branson. We didn't drive off a cliff, but we joked a lot about being Thelma and Louise. All my close friends, except Stephanie, with whom we've lost touch, were there. The keynote speaker was a young woman, born with several birth defects she attributed to her father's exposure to Agent Orange. Listening to her, Joanne and I could identify the toll it had taken among our closest friends: Joanne and Monty lost their first child to a host of birth defects. Valerie died several years ago from a type of leukemia associated with Agent Orange exposure. Liz Wilson, whose pronouncement had inspired the title of this book, had also died from Agent Orange related illnesses. Several of my nurse friends have had breast cancer. Susan has Parkinsonism, easily

L to R: Myself, Joanne with her arms around Susan. Carol is behind me, but Carol Ann is not in the picture. Reunion, 2014.

attributable to the many MEDCAPs in which she participated. Both Joanne and I have asthma.

My attitude about what I lived through in Vietnam has changed, too. I sometimes wish I could go back and tell my twenty-three-year-old self to be more positive, to consider being in Vietnam an adventure rather than a burden. Perhaps, after all, what I did in 1970 really was noble.

RIP:

Valery Biskey, RN
Charles Cochrane, MD
Ted Friedhoff, RN
Isaac Gielchinsky, MD
David Kelly, MD
Doris Ledbetter, RN
Stuart Roberts, MD
Steve Stout, Corpsman
Liz Wilson, RN

When I Die I'm Going to HEAVEN

Made in United States
Orlando, FL
05 July 2024